FOCUSED

FOCUSED

Understanding, Negotiating, and Maximizing Your Influence as a School Leader

Jim Watterston • Yong Zhao

FOR INFORMATION:

Corwin

A SAGE Company

2455 Teller Road

Thousand Oaks, California 91320

(800) 233-9936

www.corwin.com

SAGE Publications Ltd.

1 Oliver's Yard

55 City Road

London EC1Y 1SP

United Kingdom

SAGE Publications India Pvt. Ltd.

Unit No 323-333, Third Floor, F-Block

International Trade Tower Nehru Place

New Delhi 110 019

India

SAGE Publications Asia-Pacific Pte. Ltd.

18 Cross Street #10-10/11/12

China Square Central

Singapore 048423

Vice President and
  Editorial Director: Monica Eckman

Senior Acquisitions Editor: Tanya Ghans

Content Development
  Manager: Desirée A. Bartlett

Senior Editorial Assistant: Nyle De Leon

Project Editor: Amy Schroller

Copy Editor: Diana Breti

Typesetter: C&M Digitals (P) Ltd.

Proofreader: Dennis Webb

Cover Designer: Gail Buschman

Marketing Manager: Morgan Fox

Copyright © 2024 by Corwin Press, Inc.

All rights reserved. Except as permitted by U.S. copyright law, no part of this work may be reproduced or distributed in any form or by any means, or stored in a database or retrieval system, without permission in writing from the publisher.

When forms and sample documents appearing in this work are intended for reproduction, they will be marked as such. Reproduction of their use is authorized for educational use by educators, local school sites, and/or noncommercial or nonprofit entities that have purchased the book.

All third-party trademarks referenced or depicted herein are included solely for the purpose of illustration and are the property of their respective owners. Reference to these trademarks in no way indicates any relationship with, or endorsement by, the trademark owner.

Printed in the United States of America

Library of Congress Cataloging-in-Publication Data

Names: Watterston, Jim, author. | Zhao, Yong, 1965- author.

Title: Focused : understanding, negotiating, and maximizing your influence as a school leader / Jim Watterston, Yong Zhao.

Description: Thousand Oaks, California : Corwin, 2024. | Includes bibliographical references and index.

Identifiers: LCCN 2023044237 | ISBN 9781071857137 (paperback) | ISBN 9781071857144 (epub) | ISBN 9781071857151 (epub) | ISBN 9781071857120 (pdf)

Subjects: LCSH: Educational leadership. | School management and organization. | School environment.

Classification: LCC LB2806 .Z48 2024 | DDC 371.2/011—dc23/eng/20231025

LC record available at https://lccn.loc.gov/2023044237

This book is printed on acid-free paper.

24 25 26 27 28 10 9 8 7 6 5 4 3 2 1

DISCLAIMER: This book may direct you to access third-party content via Web links, QR codes, or other scannable technologies, which are provided for your reference by the author(s). Corwin makes no guarantee that such third-party content will be available for your use and encourages you to review the terms and conditions of such third-party content. Corwin takes no responsibility and assumes no liability for your use of any third-party content, nor does Corwin approve, sponsor, endorse, verify, or certify such third-party content.

CONTENTS

Prologue and Authors' Acknowledgments	xi
Publisher's Acknowledgments	xiii
About the Authors	xv
Introduction	1
The Three Stages of This Book	3
Existential Challenges	4
What Is the Job of the School Principal?	5

STAGE I: HOW TO BUILD A LEADERSHIP PARADIGM FOR OUTSTANDING SCHOOLS

1. School Leadership: Finding the Space to Do the Job Effectively	11
Great Teachers Are Not Automatically Great Leaders	12
Principals Should Only Do the Essential Work	12
The Complex Leadership Space	13
Empowerment Leadership	15
Reframe School Leadership	16
From Expert to Enabler	17
The Conductor Principal: What Empowering Leaders Do	18
Orchestral Empowerment: Sustaining School Leaders With Architecture and Infrastructure	20
Context Matters: What About Small Schools?	22
Is It Sustainable? The Work That Only the School Leader Should Do	23
Chapter 1 Focus Points	26
2. Negotiating the Inverted Triangle of Influence	27
Identify and Build Your Triangle of Influence	28
The Inverted Triangle of Influence	31
Serve the Students, Not the System	33

Empower and Trust Teachers to Make Important Decisions	35
Partner With District and Regional Offices	37
Education System Bureaucracy and Policymakers	39
Other Actors in the Triangle of Influence	39
Chapter 2 Focus Points	40

3. Leading to Create a Game Plan for Success — 41

Leading a Unique School Game Plan	44
The Game Plan: Democratizing the "Way We Do Things Around Here"	46
Creating Time and Space for Innovation and Reform	47
Working in Teams	48
Leveraging the Game Plan to Lead the Capability Building of Staff	49
Suggested Elements to Include in Strong Game Plans	52
Aligning the Learning Community	53
Chapter 3 Focus Points	55

4. Leading a Renewed Purpose of Education — 57

Create a School Culture in Which Students Are Skilled in Finding Problems	57
The Purposes of Education	60
Suggested Action Steps for Leading the New Curricula	61
Suggested Action Steps for Resolving Potential Conflicts Among Educational Outcomes	62
Assessments	66
Suggested Action Steps for Implementing Innovative Assessments	68
Suggested Action Steps for Leading the Change for a Revitalized Education	69
Chapter 4 Focus Points	71

STAGE II: WHAT ARE THE MOST INFLUENTIAL ELEMENTS FOR COLLECTIVE SUCCESS?

5. Leading Students — 75

One Size Does Not Fit All	77
Understand the Learners	78
Rethink the Value of Talent Diversity	80
The Exclusion of Students in Education Reforms	81
Suggested Action Steps for Leading Students for Students	81
Chapter 5 Focus Points	88

6. Leading Teachers and Other Players in School	89
Teachers Are the Most Important Assets in School	90
Lead Teachers as Self-Determined Individuals	91
Suggested Action Steps for Building a Proactive Team Culture	92
Suggested Action Steps for Building and Realizing a Vision With Teachers	94
Suggested Action Steps for Leading Teachers in the New Context of Education	100
Chapter 6 Focus Points	102

STAGE III: HOW TO AVOID THE PITFALLS THAT PREVENT SUCCESS

7. Leading Through Formative Accountability: Shifting the Locus of Control	105
Suggested Action Steps for Leading for More Effective Assessment	107
Meaningful Feedback	109
Suggested Action Steps for Adding Value and Minimizing Fear	110
Shared Accountability Provides Direction Through Agency	114
Formative and Summative Accountability	115
Know-How and Hope Instead of Fear and Risk Aversion	116
Chapter 7 Focus Points	117

8. Leading for Sustainability: Embracing Disruption and Crisis	119
Impactful Changes	120
Suggested Action Steps for Leading for the Future: The Changes We Must Have	125
Development and Facilitation of Responsive Changes	130
The Innovator's Dilemma	131
Chapter 8 Focus Points	132

| References | 133 |
| Index | 139 |

PROLOGUE AND AUTHORS' ACKNOWLEDGMENTS

This book is the outcome of a wonderful and enriching collaboration between Jim and Yong. We first connected a few decades ago in Australia during one of Yong's visits to provide workshops for teachers and school leaders. Over time we have built an enduring friendship and a mutual respect for each other's work and understandings, recognizing immediately that we both have very different experiences and perspectives regarding what schools and school systems should be focusing on to bring about better engagement and enhanced performance for students and teachers. Writing this book has been a rewarding learning experience for both of us.

Jim has had experiences as a teacher and a leader of schools, regions, school systems, and as a university dean. Yong's experience has primarily been in higher education as a researcher and professor. Based on these experiences, we have developed different understandings, writing styles, and ways of thinking. Our objective is to combine the insights from Jim's practical experiences working with thousands of school leaders in different Australian states with Yong's broad observations about education in the U.S., Australia, China, and various other countries.

The more we connected and conversed (occasionally over a meal and a great bottle of wine or two), the more we realized that the differences we brought to the table were complementary and aligned. Our contrasting views of the education ecosystem have converged over the years as we debated and reimagined the potential of education. We both had a desire to provide greater agency for students and teachers to reimagine teaching and learning that inspires and builds upon the passions and curiosity that everyone possesses.

In 2019 we became work colleagues at the University of Melbourne. Jim would Zoom in from Melbourne on Friday mornings and Yong would Zoom in on Thursday evening from the U.S. West Coast. These conversations created an outlet to think about educational practices that better engage students, reimagine schools where bureaucracy does not stifle innovation, and focus leadership on empowering those who are in the classroom.

The work was not smooth or easy. At first, we struggled to coherently integrate our observations and learnings into a meaningful book. We talked about our ideas, shared our stories, and doubted ourselves. We threw away many drafts and developed new ones. We learned numerous lessons and gained new insights. After more than 2 years, this writing process has eventually allowed us to integrate new macro perspectives and time-tested practical observations.

"Thursdays with Jim" and "Fridays with Yong" have been ongoing sources of educational nourishment, friendship, and humor, spiced with challenging each other's ideas and perceptions. In reading this work, you will undoubtedly identify Yong's deeply considered ideas and innovative thinking matched with Jim's diverse school leadership experiences and strategic imperatives, which hopefully connect the "yin and yang" of high-performing school leadership.

Writing this book brought back memories of great colleagues who have helped shape our ideas about leadership in education. Among them, Dr. Barbara Watterston has inspired both of us to work through our challenges when writing the book but, more important, she has contributed tremendously to our intellectual growth. Barb is an excellent education leader herself and a great educator, communicator, and facilitator. The late Dr. Richard Elmore influenced our thinking about education and educational leadership significantly, as has Dr. Michael Fullan, Professor Brian Caldwell, and Professors Andy Hargreaves and Dennis Shirley.

There are several school leaders who have influenced this book and are particularly worth mentioning. We honor the late Keith Warwick who left us too early. His outstanding school leadership is reflected in this book with a description he provided, at our request, of his school's impressive improvement trajectory, which is featured in Chapter 2. We recognize his commitment and contribution to the profession.

Patrea Walton, an iconic educator who has changed lives for the better across Queensland, Australia, is recognized for her focused leadership and her determination not to leave anyone behind. Wilma Coulton, a principal from Victoria in Australia, has always been decades ahead of her time as an inspiring leader, empowering and growing emerging leaders throughout her amazing career.

Larry Rosenstock, founding principal of High Tech High in San Diego, influenced Yong's thinking about education and school leadership. Dr. Chris Kennedy, superintendent of schools in West Vancouver, Canada, is a great example of focused leadership, as is Dr. Jim Scott, former president of Punahou School in Hawaii; Dr. Emily McCarren, Executive Head of

Keystone Academy in Beijing, China; Mr. Zhou Yinchun, principal of Number 8 Secondary School in Chongqing, China; and Gabriel Rshaid, Head of the Global School and former Headmaster of St. Andrew's Scots School in Buenos Aires, Argentina.

We dedicate this book to all school leaders who work hard for each and every student and their amazing teachers. We also dedicate this book to each other. Our lives are all the better for this friendship and collaboration.

PUBLISHER'S ACKNOWLEDGMENTS

Corwin gratefully acknowledges the contributions of the following reviewers:

Jacie Maslyk, Educational Consultant
Educator-Presenter-Author
Coraopolis, PA

Louis Lim, Principal
Bur Oak Secondary School
Markham, Ontario, Canada

Ellen Perconti, Superintendent
Goldendale School District
Goldendale, Washington

Peter Dillon, Superintendent
Berkshire Hills Regional School District
Stockbridge, Massachusetts

ABOUT THE AUTHORS

Dr. Jim Watterston

From his first job as a teacher in a rural Indigenous classroom in his home state of Western Australia to his appointment as the dean of the Faculty of Education at the University of Melbourne, Professor Jim Watterston brings more than 40 years of successful experience across a diverse range of educational roles and sectors.

Jim spent his first 10 years in the profession as a teacher before being promoted to principal in a range of primary and secondary schools. He then progressed to the role of regional director in WA and Victoria before he was appointed the deputy secretary of the Victorian Education Department and director general of both the Australian Capital Territory (ACT) and, more recently, Queensland Department of Education and Training. Jim was awarded a doctorate in education at the University of WA in 2004. He is currently the dean of the Faculty of Education at the University of Melbourne.

In addition to appointments to many education-related boards, Professor Watterston served for 6 years as the national president of the Australian Council for Education Leaders and is recognized as an influential advocate for the education sector. His contribution to education has been acknowledged both nationally and internationally with awards from a number of professional bodies and educational institutions, including the highly prestigious Ordre des Palmes Académiques (Chevalier) by the French government in 2014 for a distinguished contribution to education.

Dr. Yong Zhao

Yong Zhao is a foundation distinguished professor in the School of Education at the University of Kansas and a professor in Educational Leadership at the Melbourne Graduate School of Education in Australia. He previously served as the presidential chair, associate dean, and director of the Institute for Global and Online Education in the College of Education, University of Oregon, where he was also a professor in the Department of Educational Measurement, Policy, and Leadership. Prior to Oregon, Yong Zhao was university distinguished professor at the College of Education, Michigan State University, where he also served as the founding director of the Center for Teaching and Technology, executive director of the Confucius Institute, as well as executive director of the U.S.-China Center for Research on Educational Excellence. He is an elected member of the National Academy of Education and a fellow of the International Academy of Education. Yong Zhao has received numerous awards, including the Early Career Award from the American Educational Research Association, Outstanding Public Educator from the Horace Mann League of the USA, the Distinguished Achievement Award in Professional Development from the Association of Education Publishers, and the ACEL Nganakarrawa Award. He has been recognized as one of the most influential educational scholars. His works focus on the implications of globalization and technology on education. He has published more than 100 articles and nearly 40 books. Learn more at zhaolearning.com.

INTRODUCTION

Focus, focus, and focus! Focus is what this book is about. Here we aim to help school leaders understand what they should focus on and why. We share examples, vignettes, and practical advice to illustrate how to focus without losing sight of the big picture. School leaders often are overwhelmed (Klusmann et al., 2023). They feel they need to be responsible for everything happening in the school, from curriculum to pedagogy, from teachers to students, from finance to extracurricular activities, from the physical environments to school culture, and from systematic requirements and regulations to community relations. As a result, school leaders are tempted to do everything, which of course is impossible. In this book, we focus on what school leaders should do and how they can prioritize the most important factors for the greatest impact.

When stakeholders better understand their roles and responsibilities within the school and are laser-focused on those roles, they understand how to hold themselves accountable for producing the agreed-upon outcomes. This is a key component of every school's improvement plan, which we refer to in this book as "The Game Plan." The plan should clarify the common vision and outline the responsibilities of each role. After reading this book, we hope that school leaders will be more empowered to only do the things that matter by creating a school culture where

- Leaders empower, coach, and support others within the local school ecosystem with time and resources to improve practice, strategy, and learning for all.

- Leaders spend the overwhelming portion of their time building leadership density across the school community so that agency and expertise are shared and student focused.

- All staff have clarity in their roles and are integral and important team members who can lead future-facing, school-based innovation within an evidence-based culture where everyone thrives.

- All staff collectively develop and commit to a team-based "game plan" that critically identifies manageable workloads and *the way we all agree to do things* in our high-performing school.

- Teachers and students feel empowered to work together to develop a culture of agency in which they have the time and space to exercise self-determination, pursue purpose, personalize learning, and effectively engage as a learning community.

- Student learning is focused on students' foundations of learning, personal interests, strengths, and a mindset that will help them succeed throughout their lives.

- Leaders, teachers, and staff take collective ownership for reform and improvement in school outcomes.

- Students understand their roles and responsibilities as learners, are skilled in identifying and solving problems, participate in designing their own learning, and are involved in strategy meetings and school decision making.

We live in a world where the pace of change is rapid, disruptive, challenging, opportunistic, and leaving many people behind. Formal education has traditionally been about preparing the workers of tomorrow based on the certainty of yesterday (OECD, 2016). As diligent educators, we have previously followed the emerging trends and societal changes and cautiously adjusted, but now, as we deal globally with a multitude of existential challenges, schools, and the structure of education in general, we need to rapidly adapt to ensure learning is future-focused and centered on innovative solutions rather than consolidating practices from the past (Pelletier et al., 2023).

Although school leadership can be invigorating and rewarding, we know that it is also extremely difficult and incredibly challenging. Community and government have high expectations of school leaders and teachers are demanding, and evidence suggests that in many countries there are fewer educators prepared to take up these pivotal roles. The education profession is under duress and, arguably, being challenged like never before.

As the equity gap between students of high and low socioeconomic status continues to widen, more students are disengaging and losing their way (OECD, 2012, 2016). Therefore, it is essential that education from early childhood onward be reoriented and restructured to ensure that the change-makers, artisans, innovators, inventors, and civic leaders of tomorrow will protect and save our planet while ensuring global harmony, safety, opportunity, and equity for all.

This book provides school leaders with ideas to valiantly lead needed changes rather than continuing to respond to latent change. We desperately need global school leaders who harness the energy, drive, and commitment of their wider community to ensure that all students can invest themselves in real-world issues (UNESCO, 2021). Students need to be guided to learn anytime, anywhere—within the traditional school setting as well as outside the school fence. Each chapter opens with an **illustrative vignette**. We also share **practical examples** and **additional stories** to illustrate that with a focused approach, school leaders can ensure that students are empowered, confident, capable, and willing to solve the problems of their world. Each chapter offers substantive, research-based **suggested action steps** for becoming a more focused leader. At the end of each chapter, you will find **focus points** to support a focused approach to school leadership.

We don't use the term *focused* loosely. We don't mean structures are abandoned thoughtlessly and change is made for change's sake. Rather, we define focused bravery as a state in which the school leader understands their influence and can negotiate and maximize positive change. We advocate for the development of intentional courage to do what is right based on evidence and together with a willing coalition that is clearing the way and addressing contextual problems of practice to provide equity and success for all.

For students to succeed, high-performing school leaders must *only* do the work that only leaders can do. This book is, therefore, about what that meaningful and influential work is and what you will need to change to become a brave and focused leader. We have met and worked with thousands of school leaders who are leading high-performing teams in which everyone has agency and the license to work as a tight-knit team to lead from the front. We have seen this work. We know that this is possible and have seen that innovation and constructive change are best driven at the local level.

THE THREE STAGES OF THIS BOOK

Stage I (Chapters 1–4): How to Build a Leadership Paradigm for Outstanding Schools

The first four chapters are about a paradigm shift in leadership, with **Chapter 1** focusing on the importance of leadership and strategies to find the space and time for it. **Chapter 2** invites the reader to consider reorganizing the importance of the various players in the education system and how to bring system-level resources to support the school. **Chapter 3** discusses strategies school leaders use to build a constantly evolving democratic and comprehensive game plan for the school. **Chapter 4** discusses the multiple and potentially conflicting outcomes of education and how to lead with the ultimate purpose of education.

Stage II (Chapters 5–6): What Are the Most Influential Elements for Collective Success?

Chapter 5 discusses directions and strategies school leaders should implement to lead students in their learning and **Chapter 6** discusses how school leaders lead and support teachers and the wider school community in providing the best education for all students.

Stage III (Chapters 7–8): How to Avoid the Pitfalls That Prevent Success

Chapter 7 discusses how schools become reliant on high-stakes standardized testing and instead should focus on formative accountability, which is much more targeted and meaningful for teachers and students. **Chapter 8**, the concluding chapter, revisits the massive challenges facing schools and what leaders should do to help schools take advantage of the new opportunities in challenges and crises.

EXISTENTIAL CHALLENGES

As we grapple with massive growth and development of technology, including artificial intelligence (AI), the changing nature of employment, potentially unstoppable climate change, and rampant social media creating "fake news" and contesting evidence and research, we move into a post-pandemic landscape, and in many parts of the world, attracting teachers to the profession has become more challenging as teachers face heavy workloads and salaries that do not reflect the complexity of the job. Educators are often opting for other careers that are better remunerated with greater workplace flexibility. It seems also that fewer teachers are seeking school leadership roles, which is particularly challenging for hard-to-staff schools and isolated schools (Beng et al., 2020).

The arrival of new forms of AI such as ChatGPT marks the mainstream advancement of the Age of Smart Machines. AI is transforming society and is already forcing educators to rethink what is worth teaching in the classroom and how teaching should be conducted globally. Moreover, students require a more contemporary curriculum with agency over what, how, when, and why they learn (Zhao, 2021).

School is no longer simply about preparing for a job or a profession. Educators must rethink the purpose of education and how we deliver those outcomes by better engaging students and teachers (Hunter et al., 2022). A new social movement that focuses on social justice, personalization, fluid sexuality, and multicultural relationships has brought tensions to schools and society in general.

A reorganization of globalization is being forged with the division of new groups of nations. Geopolitical tensions and outbreaks of war along with Western challenges to democracy as we know it are creating deep anxiety, with many young people on edge, feeling a sense of destabilization and hopelessness (OECD, 2020).

Climate change is having a devastating impact across the world, and there is very little evidence that we are collectively and effectively addressing this threat (IPCC, 2022). Current geopolitical disputes, global economic challenges, and significantly higher cost of living mean that many families are under intense financial pressure, which brings social unrest and discontent, increased crime, and impoverishment for many.

The decline in students' social and emotional well-being globally is adding to teachers' loads because well-being has become an additional component for teachers to prioritize and deal with.

WHAT IS THE JOB OF THE SCHOOL PRINCIPAL?

Faced with these massive constraints and barriers, schools and school leaders need to stop and evaluate to change how they operate. Schools are nested in a system composed of policymakers, system leaders, quality monitors, students, parents, teachers, and many external players. Many school leaders think they are too busy with the day-to-day challenges of operating schools to have the time to consider changes to the structures and traditions of the past. They also feel constrained by bureaucratic and regressive systems, policies, and parental concerns. To lead internal reform is necessary, but it also requires focus. In this book we advocate that school leaders must be focused on the high-value work within and across their community to reorient their school to prepare students for a life of uncertainty and opportunities in an age of smart machines.

So, what should focused principals do? How do principals know what to focus on? These are some of the most challenging and contested questions regarding school leaders because there are many, and often too many, things school principals currently do but perhaps don't need to do. Learning to prioritize and FOCUS on what matters is essential for effective school leadership.

What Is the Most Effective Use of Your Time and Expertise?

During a period of lockdown in the early days of COVID-19, Jim was facilitating an online meeting of a task force of high-profile school leaders invited by their state education department in Australia to provide ongoing advice and expertise on the development of a more contemporary and relevant principal job description. They were tasked with identifying the most meaningful actions and role parameters that school leaders should prioritize to be most effective. This work had been initiated because local school leadership organizations believed that the work of the school leader was overwhelming and underresourced, and thus was not attractive

(Continued)

(Continued)

to potential applicants. Principals felt that the state school system was too "top down," which constrained innovation and did not consider the diversity and unique challenges that differentiated each school.

Toward the end of the months-long process, an eloquent and committed leader of a very large school was speaking online about how challenging it was that bureaucracies outside of the school did not understand the plight or community expectations of the school leader. Virtually mid-sentence and with a sharp rise in tone, he rapidly explained that he urgently had to leave the meeting. Everyone was naturally concerned that something very serious had required his immediate attention, but the meeting continued without him.

It was relayed the next day that the reason the leader left the meeting was that he had been told that a student had been injured in a sporting contest. The injury turned out to be a minor cut above his eye. Like others, this leader had directed his staff to always advise him immediately so that he could personally manage and be accountable for all emergencies and such issues. It is ironic that he left the meeting in the midst of explaining how his role was almost untenable because he had to be all things to all people.

This story illustrates why many school leaders find their jobs to be burdensome and overwhelming. When we have shared this story with other school leaders, the immediate response from a significant number of them has been, "Well, who else would be able to take control?" or "Of course, the school leader must be accountable for everything that happens!"

This book is designed to enable school leaders to provide their own answers to the questions "Who else will do this?" and "Who else could also be accountable?" or "How can I still be accountable without having to be everywhere?" Consequently, we focus on what we consider to be the two essential foundations of highly effective school leadership:

1. How does the school leader identify, preserve, and navigate their leadership space when the reality is that they are being pulled in every direction during the school day?

2. What is the job that only the school leader can and should be doing and what should you stop doing to ensure that you can focus on the things that matter most?

This book is not just a novel new take on school leadership. Rather, it is a book that demonstrates that effective leadership is dependent on place and context. It is a book that focuses on the interactions between the leader and the system. It is a realization that school leaders must explore, discover, and define their place in the system in order to create the space where they can effectively lead.

We chose to write this book because finding school leaders' place in the system has, to our knowledge, not overtly been discussed and deconstructed because rarely have researchers or practitioners had the lived experience of school and system leadership and been challenged by the interaction of all actors at all levels of the education hierarchy. The demands on school leaders from all directions are often overpowering, and this book identifies how to negotiate a space for school leaders to influence, advocate, empower, and create conditions for success within an educational ecosystem that can be crowded and excessively hard to navigate.

> *[This] is a book that focuses on the interactions between the leader and the system. It is a realization that school leaders must explore, discover, and define their place in the system in order to create the space where they can effectively lead.*

The space for effective school leadership is obtained through proactive interaction with the various players in the system and understanding the historical conditions of the school—and it is contingent upon the personal characteristics and awareness of the school leader. Finding the space where optimal leadership and influence take place is fundamental to the success of the leader and the school. This space is co-created by the school principal and other actors in and outside the school.

Negotiating and co-creating the space requires the school leader to have a clear understanding of the system; the players in the system; the context, history, and local conditions; and the collaboration of people in the local school community. Thus, when we encourage educators to take on a school leadership role, we must also challenge and support those appointees to look very hard to identify, understand, and carve out an optimal space and time where one can best influence and sustain positive changes.

> *Negotiating and co-creating the space requires the school leader to have a clear understanding of the system; the players in the system; the context, history, and local conditions; and the collaboration of people in the local school community.*

STAGE I

HOW TO BUILD A LEADERSHIP PARADIGM FOR OUTSTANDING SCHOOLS

CHAPTER 1

....

SCHOOL LEADERSHIP
Finding the Space to Do the Job Effectively

What Is the Job of the School Principal?

Yong was recently in conversation with a new principal of an online school. When Yong asked him what his job was, the principal was both challenged and intrigued by this question and became quite curious about what his job should really be. He laid out many things he was considering, such as appropriate use of funds, hiring and supporting quality staff, ensuring availability and use of resources, making sure that students are supported, professional development, leadership development, and creating and supporting a productive culture of learning. It is difficult to say whether these are things the principal should do without knowing the history, the culture, the staff, the students, and the systemic context of the school. So, Yong asked him to identify the things in his school that only the school principal can and should do. This vignette is meant to illustrate that few principals have had the opportunity to dive deeply into their leadership because of the overwhelming number of tasks they feel that they have to do. It is fundamental, however, that school leaders refrain from doing the work of others; instead, they need to focus almost exclusively on the tasks that build agency, teamwork, and innovation across the school community. School leaders cannot do it all, so their influence and impact are about bringing out the best in others.

There is a massive amount of scholarship on school leadership. A simple Google search of "leadership" resulted in 4,810,000,000 hits. A search for "school leadership" resulted in 1,130,000,000 hits. These resources purport to tell school leaders what they should do and what style of leader they need to be, assuming that school leaders have the freedom to be in complete control of their school and can do whatever they like. This book, however, is focused on how to navigate a school's crowded leadership space in a complex ecosystem where leaders must align the decisions of many actors, inside and outside of the school gate, to bring about improved outcomes for all students.

GREAT TEACHERS ARE NOT AUTOMATICALLY GREAT LEADERS

School leadership is not a solitary practice, and there are elements of this demanding job over which the school leader has very little control. Although an overwhelming number of school leaders are promoted from the classroom, highly effective school leadership requires an additional range of specialized administrative knowledge, specific competencies, and systemic understandings. It also requires vision, resilience, persistence, innovation, and the ability to build teams. Not everybody who comes into the principal position brings the prerequisite capabilities and the lessons learned through leadership experience. It can often be a case of learning on the job rather than being well prepared.

Great teachers don't automatically turn into high-performing school leaders because school leadership roles also require an elevated understanding of the organizational elements, structural challenges, and game-changing opportunities available. School leadership is much more than being a great teacher and understanding children, although those attributes are important. Highly effective school leaders know which levers to pull and, most important, what they must stop doing to enable them to prioritize leading others to success. Being an expert in everything and all things to all people is both impossible and undesirable, but it can become an occupational hazard for those moving into educational leadership roles.

PRINCIPALS SHOULD ONLY DO THE ESSENTIAL WORK

School leaders should only do the essential work that high-achieving school leaders undertake; they are neither responsible for doing everything nor for everyone, but they are accountable to those above for school performance. Outstanding leaders build empowered and exceptional teams in which accountability is shared, and members of the team have clear roles and an expectation that they will innovate and collectively improve outcomes. Great school leaders don't "instruct" or "distribute" work to subordinates; they mentor and support. Great leaders don't do the work of others, otherwise, they would spend a significant proportion of their time providing all of the decisions and solutions and team members would not develop, innovate, or feel empowered.

School leaders, like brilliant leaders in every field of endeavor, must understand that to be successful, they must focus on the unique work that only the leader can do. Too many school leaders, however, are overwhelmed by seemingly never-ending challenges and often menial tasks they take on, which deplete the necessary energy and capacity to stay on top of issues that make the essential difference. There is an art to great school leadership that cannot be formularized or packaged, despite a plethora of books telling you otherwise. School leadership needs to be nurtured by developing a better understanding of the limitations and opportunities inherent in the role. Leaders also need to know who else needs to be engaged and supported to be able to provide the necessary agency, innovation, and opportunity to lead effectively.

THE COMPLEX LEADERSHIP SPACE

What work should a school leader do in their leadership "space" and how should they prioritize their time to be truly effective? This is perhaps the most fundamental question all school leaders must consider when making significant changes, in order to have a positive, long-term impact on the school. Answers for many may initially seem self-evident; however, the reality is more complex, challenging, and regularly contested. In addition, the answers can change dramatically depending on whom you ask or where one sits in the education system hierarchy.

Numerous school leadership books propose leadership strategies, identify preferred leadership styles, and create schemes for leaders to enact based upon the premise that leaders have the expertise, individual freedom, and capacity to do whatever they like without due consideration of the system, the school, the community, and other players who have an external or internal vested interest. Many have also promoted the idea that school leaders are, or should be, the ultimate change agents who can take drastic action. There are many books that focus on the internal reasons why making innovative changes within schools can be so challenging. A considerable number of books discuss the deeply entrenched education system that resists changes, the complex organization of schools, and the many professionals playing intertwined roles. As a result, a school leader may succumb to the false dichotomy that either they should lead the reform of the whole organization or believe that prevailing impediments cannot be changed. The reality is, however, that school leaders cannot sustainably change or preserve anything on their own because they are performing in a complex educational ecosystem with many internal and external players who each have their own views, expectations, and deep history.

> *Leaders most certainly can and do make a difference, but it is within a complex system. The key is to find and negotiate supportive relationships across the ecosystem to ensure that all change is team driven, resourced, promoted, understood, collaborative, and, most important, protected at all levels.*

We contend that the most overlooked and fundamental element of successful school leadership is understanding and negotiating the crowded leadership landscape where the influence of many external and internal stakeholders significantly affects the opportunity for school leaders to make a difference. Leaders most certainly can and do make a difference, but it is within a complex system. The key is to find and negotiate supportive relationships across the ecosystem to ensure that all change is team driven, resourced, promoted, understood, collaborative, and, most important, protected at all levels.

The optimal place for high-performance school leadership exists in every school, but it is not blind to any leadership style. Different leaders have their own qualities, motivations, personalities, and leadership styles; however, success is driven by the prioritization of an achievable strategy that is inclusively developed and implemented by those with vested interests: teachers, students, and parents. The right leadership appointment means the perfect match between the leader and the context. Helping leaders to understand themselves, the myriad of external influences, and the wider education context is an underrated and misunderstood challenge. These extensive and powerful external influences significantly impact internal school strategic planning and implementation and must be identified, cultivated, and harnessed to ensure successful and sustainable change.

Every school principal aspires to improve their school (Bush & Glover, 2014). Every school aims to hire the best possible candidate for the principalship, but the outcome of these selection processes does not always translate to better practices, harmony, improved outcomes, or supported leadership. Despite the best of intentions, why is it that there are so many schools that have not seen significant improvement over time? Why is it that school principals do not always realize sustained improvement that continues long after their departure?

Every school's performance is impacted by a vast range of internal and external leaders, influencers, and stakeholders despite the traditional model that holds the school principal accountable for the organization's success or failure. School leaders must respond to community issues and demands, government policy, decisions and legislation, and systemic directives to build an aligned coalition to bring about success.

At all levels of the education ecosystem there are leaders and executives who have an impact on school strategy and performance. Sitting above the school leadership are people in the mid-level or top-level of bureaucracies whose responsibilities include leading, funding, and quite often directing schools within their jurisdictions. Policymakers are leaders and influencers of entire systems. Other factors that influence school performance include mandated external assessments that measure educational quality and student competencies against educational standards; textbook publishers and technology providers; and national and state curriculum frameworks (Harris & Jones, 2018).

Almost everyone in the education system has an opportunity to influence the operation of schools, but there is little recognition in the literature or in practice of these pervasive influences and their relationship to school leaders—and, consequently, the teaching staff. School leaders often feel that external stakeholders are crowding their space and constraining their opportunity to develop bespoke solutions to problems of practice. The basis for successful principal leadership is the identification, negotiation, and understanding of decision-making agency (Hattie, 2023). Although everyone can voice opinions on any aspect of the system, it is only within a specific space that the school leader can engineer substantive and realistic changes to improve performance.

EMPOWERMENT LEADERSHIP

For several decades, we have been privileged to work alongside thousands of school leaders throughout the world, and rarely have we come across people who lack the passion and energy required; however, it is obvious that high-performing school leadership requires more than simply long hours, passion, and hard work.

We have found that high-achieving school leaders are those who base their leadership on empowering others in order to build the density of leadership across the team. It is important to state up front, however, that empowering others, for us, is not a "leadership style" or a "work design principle." It is the foundation upon which successful leadership is built. It is about growing a united and constantly improving team in which everybody is recognized and supported to be their best selves.

> *The high-achieving school leaders are those who base their leadership on empowering others in order to build the density of leadership across the team.*

School leaders begin empowering others by changing their own behaviors and actions. Leave your phone and laptop in your office as you move about the school, implicitly trusting others, embracing misfires, giving people as many chances as they need, learning alongside your team, and asking more questions than you answer. Casual conversations in the corridor with teachers and students are essential opportunities to embed trust and proactive accessibility as well as to learn about others and how they work.

Empowerment is, however, hard and highly skilled work. It requires total prioritization, focus, discipline, and the framing of traditional practices as opportunities to strategically turn "lemons into lemonade." High-achieving school leaders park their egos to achieve school goals through the agency of others. Most of all, however, they are patient and celebrate school problems of practice as collective opportunities to be seized (OECD, 2018). The best leaders align events happening around them by mentoring and coaching in the moment.

To identify the essence of what we mean by empowering others, we refer to the work of Abraham Maslow who, in a paper on human motivation in 1943, proposed his hierarchy of needs psychological theory. Maslow's theory is that individuals' basic (physiological and safety) needs must be met before they will be motivated to achieve higher-level (psychological and self-fulfillment) needs. The apex of personal growth is the realization of one's full potential. If a school's staff do not have their basic needs met, then Maslow's theory would hold that they will be unable to move beyond the basic level and will ultimately not reach a state of self-actualization. Empowerment is, therefore, about helping and encouraging others to fully develop and grow their influence (Robinson & Gray, 2019). It is about building a safe and inclusive school environment in which people are trusted and supported to work together to bring about success for all.

High-performing school leaders are artisans who give their team agency and bring out the best in others through coaching and mentoring to build capability and capacity. They encourage innovation, recognize the expertise of others, and provide opportunities for them to lead on projects and priority initiatives. They are focused, brave, inclusive, collaborative, and always learning, but they don't take the limelight all the time, preferring often to work behind the scenes when empowering others. They see potential in everyone, but they set and maintain achievable standards to ensure that each person is formatively accountable for their actions. Great school leaders draw on the whole village to achieve success for all. Most important, high-performing leaders don't do other people's jobs; they do only the work that the leader should do by selectively engaging in the tasks that are the most influential and meaningful, to share the improvement of practice with all.

REFRAME SCHOOL LEADERSHIP

What is the work that high-achieving empowered school leaders prioritize? High-performing school leaders require a range of skills to ensure that the preconditions for enhanced student performance are in place, including identifying, attracting, retaining, growing, and re-energizing great talent. In a study from the Organization for Economic Co-operation and Development (OECD), Schleicher (2012) describes the fundamental role of school leaders as setting a vision and enhancing the capacities of the school community to achieve it. Similarly, other studies have identified core leadership practices exercised by principals including building a shared vision and setting directions, understanding and developing people, redesigning the organization, and managing the teaching and learning program (Leithwood et al., 2006).

The dominant conceptual model of contemporary school leadership needs to be reframed. The term *instructional leader* emerged in the late 1970s during a push for principals to return to their roots and focus on directing curriculum implementation to teachers and general staff members. Firestone and Robinson (2010) contend,

Abstract constructs like transformational leadership and instructional leadership provide only the most general guidance to people in schools about what they need to do in order to help schools improve. While sensitive to varying degrees to school conditions, they are rather insensitive to teaching *per se*.

Arguably, this was a time when there was a binary notion of school leadership: principals either focused on organizational management or focused on leading teaching and learning. The instructional leadership model has been invoked by many, including practitioners, with school principals directly assuming the leadership of the curriculum, pedagogy, and assessment elements of the school's practice, along with all aspects of management, policy development, and implementation (Hattie, 2023).

Today, however, high-performing school leaders have moved beyond the ideal of an accomplished expert principal who leads all aspects of teaching and learning in addition to the complex managerial aspects of the role (Australian Institute for Teaching and School Leadership [AITSL], 2014). They have moved to a more contemporary and sustainable leadership role that places a significantly greater emphasis on the leader as a builder and enabler of empowered teams. We believe that the traditional model of one person being ultimately accountable for school leadership is both unsustainable and impractical in the constantly evolving educational landscape. As Fiarman (2017) states in *Building a Schoolwide Leadership Mindset: How Can We Create School Cultures in Which Everyone Shares Responsibility?* "As school leaders, we have to place more value on cultivating others' skills and insights than on demonstrating our own expertise" (p. 24).

Such a transition, however, requires much more than a conceptual shift from school leaders. Ultimately, it must also be underpinned by structural, cultural, administrative, and organizational shifts from governments and bureaucracies to move single-point accountability from the "hero" leader to that of an empowered high-functioning leadership team.

FROM EXPERT TO ENABLER

In today's complex and challenging environment, it is unsustainable to be an expert instructional leader in all domains across a school (Ainley et al., 2022). We believe that it is well past time for the school leader to be considered an empowering leader, rather than the all-consuming instructional leader. We must stop expecting school leaders to be the experts in everything when what schools really need is a skilled leader who builds high-quality, informed, and empowered teams based on a shared vision.

The empowerment of others, as a school leadership mainstay, is an unambiguous departure from the traditional notions of delegation, which can cause school leaders to feel compelled to directly manage subordinates while retaining end-of-line responsibility and accountability. Empowered teams include capable, well-prepared, and supported team members in recognized portfolio leadership roles with formative accountability, which capitalizes on the individual's emerging expertise.

As integral members of an empowered leadership team, staff are valued for their expertise, which in turn increases their sense of agency and encourages collective decision making. In this model, decisions and prioritization are a collective enterprise in which all views are considered. Empowerment, therefore, builds confidence, reliability, and trust in the organization because power is democratized and decision making is more localized and contextualized. Most important, empowerment shares the load, builds positive leadership experience, and facilitates organizational succession planning through identified career pathways.

The high-performing educational leader draws on their experience and know-how to lead as a role model, coach, supporter, and mentor of a high-functioning team of portfolio experts who are empowered to lead through genuine interdependency and mutual accountability. The success of an empowering school leader lies in recognizing the interconnectedness of mindsets, policies, and processes that contribute to and inform quality leadership development and practice.

Sharratt and Planche (2016) in *Leading Collaborative Learning: Empowering Excellence*, argue that collaborative learning is key to improving leadership and teaching. They posit that collaboration is more complex than simply "working together" and that parity (all parties in the collaboration have some power) and reciprocity (leaders and followers believing they are receiving mutual benefit for their efforts) are vital ingredients. Importantly, they point to school leadership teams possessing the knowledge, skills, and practices related to purposeful collaboration with a commitment to improvement; agreed norms and protocols; and a culture of trust, mutual respect, and strong working relationships, all of which contribute to improving outcomes.

THE CONDUCTOR PRINCIPAL: WHAT EMPOWERING LEADERS DO

Education research shows that the multitude of school variables, when considered separately, have little effect on learning (Hattie, 2012, 2023). The real payoff comes when individual variables combine to reach a critical mass, creating the conditions under which that can occur is the job of the school leader (Wallace Foundation, 2013). The role of an empowering school principal is analogous to that of an orchestral conductor, with facilitative power exercised not over but through others. A conductor empowers and unites the musicians through an authentic collaboration that sustains the high-performing orchestra. As Luce (1992) concludes, "When principals (school leaders) provide teachers with what is needed, three things usually happen: staff members are empowered to participate; staff members take ownership; and better decisions are made by the people who are best suited to make them" (p. 6).

Ainley (2019) says that the leadership required to empower teams to develop and continually improve their collective performance is leadership that is based on listening, supporting, and coaching. He contrasts this with leadership based on observation, measurement, and intervention, which limits team cohesiveness.

The conductor leads the orchestral performance, but the individual musicians contribute their unique talents and expertise as required. Conductors don't usually play any instrument during the performance; their role is to bring all players together to be the best that they can be as a collective. Every member of the orchestra requires the leadership of the conductor to synchronize their unique talents and contribute to a successful outcome. Like a masterful conductor, an empowering school leader is primarily concerned with the overall performance, not with being an expert in every aspect of the process. A critical component of the role of "conductor principal" is enabling and empowering a high-functioning team through the provision of collaborative feedback and mentoring.

> *A critical component of the role of "conductor principal" is enabling and empowering a high-functioning team through the provision of collaborative feedback and mentoring.*

In short, the unique expertise of the "conductor school principal" is the ability to unite and lead the team, not to do it all. Linda Darling-Hammond, in providing a scholar's view of the principal-teacher connection, also draws on the conductor analogy in describing the work of an empowering school leader:

> A lot of a principal's work can be invisible to teachers when they're in the classroom. I often use the metaphor of the conductor of the orchestra. We watch the conductor, we're in the audience, and we say, "I could do that. Piece of cake. Right?" That's true of teachers' skill in the classroom; it's also true of principals' skill in orchestrating the collective, harmonious work of teachers.
> (in Wallace Foundation, 2013, pp. 19–20)

It is essential, therefore, to design school leadership structures that are built on the differential expertise of well-prepared and high-performing team members. Such a conceptual shift requires school systems and policymakers to think very differently about the resourcing, preparation, ongoing professional development, accountability processes, and, most important, the position descriptions of the key positions required in school leadership teams. Focusing on the team over self means maximizing everyone's talents, which leads to sustainable results (Kirtman & Fullan, 2016).

CHAPTER 1 • SCHOOL LEADERSHIP

The traditional and well-accepted notion of appointing a school leader to run a school while delegating or distributing some tasks to others is outdated. In the team-based contemporary model of school leadership, leaders may not be deep content experts in every subject area, but they can be instrumental in guiding teaching by asking effective questions, providing shared and differentiated professional learning opportunities, using tools of observation and evaluation effectively, and supporting teacher leaders (Ippolito & Fisher, 2019).

The picture that emerges from talking with school leaders is that although they want to make a difference in their school communities, for many it is impossible to balance the excessive demands of an exclusive model of leadership, interpreted by many as being the expert leader in all areas. Many describe their roles as isolating, unending, dependent, frustrating, misunderstood, and exhausting. To address a conceptual redesign of the school leadership role, we must ask, "What could principals realistically change?" and "What would they be prepared to give up to empower other members of a collaborative leadership team?"

It is easy to call for a conceptual change to the role of a school leader, but as those in the field will undoubtedly be quick to point out, how do we conduct an orchestra when we are short on well-prepared musicians?

ORCHESTRAL EMPOWERMENT: SUSTAINING SCHOOL LEADERS WITH ARCHITECTURE AND INFRASTRUCTURE

Enabling school leaders to lead successful organizational transformations requires much more than a reconceptualized leadership construct and a cute "conductor leadership" metaphor. Ultimately, it requires dedicated understanding, agreement, and action from governments, bureaucracies, and the myriad of educational stakeholders, including professional associations, researchers, and the public. It also certainly requires a clear articulation by the school leader of the leadership model and the buy-in required across the school. It is fundamental that when people are talking to a member of an empowered school leadership team (who isn't the school leader) they know they are talking to a trusted senior change maker who has influence and can make things happen.

To move to an empowering leadership model, schools need to allocate resources and time to add expert educational leaders to established teams, depending on the size and complexity of the school. Portfolio areas may include teaching and learning, assessment and reporting, behavior management, corporate services, resource deployment, well-being, diversity and inclusion, community engagement, innovation and research, and subschool directors, in the case of fractional appointments. All staff could conceivably be part of the leadership through subcommittee appointments, so that decision making is democratized and shared across the school. Not only do a number of these appointments need to be part of a school's leadership profile, but team members need to be respected by bureaucracies as decision makers who can attend relevant meetings and speak for the school, instead of the traditional overreliance on the school principal, who is deemed to be the influential keeper of all knowledge and authority.

Of course, developing the capacity of an empowered leadership team requires a systemic commitment to specialized professional development and quality preparation programs that focus on areas such as relevant content, policy and legislation, career stage development, and the development of high-performance teams. Ensuring that each school has a functioning and high-performing "orchestra" will enable the principal to focus on expert conducting rather than trying to play every instrument. As noted by AITSL (2019), "Diverse, quality school leadership teams improve school performance, increase innovation, and provide more creative approaches to problem solving" (p. 3).

Table 1.1 articulates the contemporary school leadership transition required to revitalize and sustain principals at this critical time of need.

TABLE 1.1 FROM INSTRUCTIONAL TO EMPOWERING; A NEW LEADERSHIP PARADIGM

TRADITIONAL INSTRUCTIONAL LEADERSHIP PRACTICE	AN EMPOWERING SCHOOL LEADERSHIP MODEL
Single point of accountability	A diverse and emerging leadership team with shared accountability
Generic leadership professional development (one size fits all)	On-site training with ongoing career stage renewal (personalization)
Single reference point for all problem solving (sole responsibility)	Team members are empowered with end-of-line authority to make collaborative decisions (mutual responsibility)
Closely managed delegation to subordinates	Leader serves as a mentor and coach to support collaborative team-based capability development
Principal-only attendance at external meetings and briefings with senior line managers	External stakeholders embrace an expert-based team approach where expertise is portfolio driven
Insurmountable exclusive principal workload	Greater focus on the "conductor" role with emphasis on coaching and building leadership capability in others
School leader is accountable and accessible to all stakeholders (Lone Ranger)	Collective problem solving among an empowered team (leadership diversity)
"Full-service" instructional leader leading teaching and learning, pedagogy, and assessment	Expert leadership team based on specific portfolio knowledge and capability
Ad-hoc leadership succession planning	Internal leadership pathways, identification, and dedicated progression support

CONTEXT MATTERS: WHAT ABOUT SMALL SCHOOLS?

School leaders in smaller schools, however, won't be able to "lead and conduct a full-sized orchestra" if systems don't allocate proportionate time for additional portfolio leadership roles to ensure that we don't continue to place total accountability and expectation on the Lone Ranger full-service leader. Although a growing number of small to medium-sized schools have fractional allocations or appointments to roles such as deputy or assistant principals, heads of department, business managers, and teacher leaders, there needs to be a greater focus on providing resources to ensure empowered leadership team capacity in small schools.

Harness the Skills of Everyone

Jim's first leadership role was in a small rural school with only 36 students. He found that the only way to manage effectively was to share the leadership responsibilities between the two full-time teachers (himself and one other), the part-time teacher, and the school's business manager and gardener. The five of them recognized that they each had different skills, interests, and experiences, so they quickly agreed that a shared decision-making approach would empower all of them to make better decisions. They also had a school council who, as part of this approach, were empowered as an integral part of the leadership team to manage and lead the engagement and connection with all parents and community members. The benefit of this shared approach was that all stakeholders in this very small school were provided with agency in decision making through shared goals and aspirations. Jim did not abandon his leadership responsibility; he made sure that the skills of all others were harnessed and deployed as a meaningful and cohesive team.

Most schools, including smaller schools, are also served at various levels by external positions, such as district or area coordinators, visiting psychologists, and allied health workers, in addition to regional or system officers who work in a range of schools, such as school improvement coordinators and curriculum support officers. For many leaders of small schools, these support services are often "done to" the school and not always "done with" or as a part of the school, so in an empowering leadership transformation, it will be fundamental that visiting providers and experts become a part of an empowered internal leadership team. In this model, the locus of control, from a school improvement perspective, resides within the school rather than in so-called expert external guidance. Re-badging external providers, bureaucratic and regional staff, and non-teaching staff such as the business manager as leadership team members requires more than new labeling.

To build effective teams, reciprocity and mutual responsibility are key. As an integral element of meaningful structural and cultural change, it will be essential for all service providers and those within the school with allied responsibilities to receive leadership training and ongoing collective professional development and mentoring related to working in an interdisciplinary team.

It is also possible for school systems to rethink the leadership structures of small schools by appointing a more senior school leader who mentors, supports, and coaches a group of smaller schools in a "hub and spoke" leadership model that is empowering to those in the school while at the same time building a larger team-based leadership collaboration across the school collective. Such structures build alignment, facilitate career development, and sustain practices that will address the multiple challenges currently faced by principals in isolated and under-resourced locations.

IS IT SUSTAINABLE? THE WORK THAT ONLY THE SCHOOL LEADER SHOULD DO

Undoubtedly, the school leader must lead and be present; however, many leaders feel the need to do it all. Their car is the first one in the parking lot in the morning and the last to leave in the evening. It turns out that the more they do, the more they feel they must do. For a growing number, it is becoming unsustainable as we find more senior leaders leaving the profession.

Although school leaders could argue that their salary is not reflective of the importance of the role and accountabilities, in almost all cases they are the highest-paid employee on site. So how do we get the best value for money from the school leader and what does that work look like? The following list comes from our ongoing observations and conversations with school leaders:

Suggested Action Steps for Being a Focused School Leader

- Spend time "on the balcony" observing and building a deep understanding of the school culture while making sure that systems are in place and that they work without being dependent on the leader (Heifetz & Linsky, 2002).

- Understand and appreciate what others do and how well they do it. Liberally provide acknowledgment, praise, and constructive advice to empower those across the leadership team. People don't want their leader to tell them what to do; they want their leader to know what they do and to help them to do it better. Recognizing the talent in others is the foundation for creating a culture of empowerment.

- Attract and provide time and resources to enable other leaders to innovate and improve practice.

- Lead the collegiate development and facilitation of the school's organizational game plan, which identifies "the way we do things around here."

- Spend time engaging with external and internal stakeholders to build relationships, alignment, and an understanding of the empowered leadership model.

- Build and identify leadership capability and density in all others, including those without a formal leadership position. Ensure that everyone's leadership contribution is visible, supported, and appreciated.

- Act as the gatekeeper to ensure staff are not distracted by unnecessary activity and commitments that don't make a difference.

- Ensure that all staff are effectively guided and supported to be their best. This particularly includes staff who may initially be disengaged or dispirited. Finding ways to get them on board means understanding their motivation and interests and finding out how their passion can be renewed. It also means supporting colleagues during times of personal stress, illness, and family issues.

THE WORK THAT THE SCHOOL LEADER SHOULD STOP DOING

If school leaders are going to lead in the ways that have been described above, then as the title of this book suggests, they need to be completely focused on the things that need to be done and stop doing things that others can do or no longer need doing. It's clear that for a leader to be effective, they don't just add more tasks or roles to their current job description. When we ask school leaders what they should stop doing, the answers usually finish with, "Well who'll do the work if I don't do it? Everyone is too busy to take on MY jobs!"

> *Not all of what you are currently doing needs to be given to other people. There are some things that need to be divested, reprioritized, or rethought.*

Our answer (which does not always evoke a positive response) is that not all of what you are currently doing needs to be given to other people. There are some things that need to be divested, reprioritized, or rethought. The following list may stimulate deeper conversations about what leaders need to let go.

Suggested Action Steps for What Focused School Leaders Can Stop Doing

- Stop leading everything. Let others take the lead in their areas of expertise and be prepared to give them room to do it their way and in-time support.

- Stop being the Lone Ranger and savior for every crisis event. Work as a team assign functions and portfolios to others and focus on the group or school's response. Trust others to be able to manage issues within their portfolios. Let others chair committees and develop strategies across the school, but do not stop attending and participating in the group.

- Stop teaching classes and being part of the playground roster (as much as you might love it!). Your class is now the staff in your school, and you need to coach and mentor them.

- Use technology to support your coaching and mentoring, such as video vignettes, school-based webinars, and opportunities to work online with colleagues in other like-minded schools. Demonstrate what success looks like with exemplary practice. Seek effective teaching and learning within the school and share this with staff.

- Stop being the first in and the last to leave. Demonstrate to your team that you have a work/life balance and that it is OK for them to have one as well.

- Stop failing the pronoun test by using "I," "my," and "me" and start using "we," "us," and "our." It makes an amazing difference.

- Stop doing your office "leadership work" and attending all external meetings while other staff are engaged in collaborative learning experiences. You must be the change that you want others to make.

- Stop talking so much. Talk less, show that you understand, and listen more.

The problem is—like it or not—great teachers who are promoted into leadership positions are accustomed to having to do a multitude of tasks. As newly appointed school leaders, many continue to put pressure on themselves to prove that they can and will continue to do it all. To ensure that a school leader does only the work the leader should do is an extraordinary and highly challenging proposition that ultimately can only be resolved by the leaders themselves.

Our observations over time are that high-performing school leaders have proactively resolved this question and it has made a positive impact on their schools' performance and outcomes. They don't do less work at the expense of their colleagues. They just do more of the most impactful work and capability building to empower others. We know that some do not agree with this analogy, but schools, like businesses, are judged by the quality of their service delivery. In the business world that means face-to-face interaction and quality of customer service are the key, with the equivalent in schools being the connectedness of the teaching and learning and the whole student experience as the lens by which the school is judged.

Although leadership is vitally important to the success of any school, communities judge their schools by how well their children are taught and nurtured. School leaders, therefore, need to recognize that teachers are the primary force of change in schools because they deal directly with students.

Teachers are the most prized and important resources in your school, and they need to know that. We saw this during the COVID-19 pandemic when schools were locked down during long periods of quarantine. Teachers, globally, without any warning and mostly without prior experience, transitioned to online or remote learning in innovative and unique ways to continue to engage students and support families in desperate times. Never has there been better or more universal evidence of the innate leadership, creativity, and innovation of the teaching profession. Empowering leaders are continuing to drive proactive change through the leadership of teachers.

Great coaches are only as good as their players' performance because the coach doesn't usually get to play in the game. To a lesser extent, the same applies to school leaders. In every school, there are teachers who strive to be the best they can be to enable students to develop a love of learning; however, some teachers may be more able and proactive than others. But for an entire school to make significant, impactful, and lasting changes, the school leader must provide a model of supportive and empowered leadership that impacts everyone.

This leadership is not a command-and-control job assignment. It is not directing teachers to do a simple job. Instead, this leadership is about empowering every teacher to make the changes that have been collectively agreed upon.

CHAPTER 1 FOCUS POINTS

1. A school principal's job is not to do everything. Instead, the principal should focus on the things that only the principal can do and should do. Seek sustainable ways to be impactful and effective.

2. Schools work in a complex education system involving many players. The principal needs to understand the limitations and constraints of the external systems and bureaucracy from outside of the school gate and enable all involved to work for the school. This is expanded upon in Chapter 2.

3. A principal does not need to be the expert in everything in the school. Instead, the principal is the enabler of others. Trust and support others to invest the freedom you have provided for classroom-based innovation.

CHAPTER 2

....

NEGOTIATING THE INVERTED TRIANGLE OF INFLUENCE

In this chapter, we emphasize the importance of school leaders identifying and building strong relationships with key influencers both inside and outside their school community. These influencers can either support or block the school's progress.

The *triangle of influence* is understood by most as a hierarchy with system leaders at the top and students at the bottom. This traditional concept of a triangle of influence represents a top-down model of control; however, we advocate flipping it to place students at the apex, arguing that every action taken in a school must be focused on improving student engagement and performance. Below the students in this hierarchy are the teachers, who provide direct services to students, then the district and regional offices, and finally the educational system leaders, policymakers, and government agencies at the base of the hierarchy. This flipped approach provides a bottom-up operating model whereby students and teachers are prioritized as the school's empowered agents of change and innovation.

Inverting the triangle offers a perspective shift from the traditional model of line management, in which teachers and school leaders are subservient to external leaders and influencers, to a model that values those most directly engaged in teaching and learning. We argue this approach to school improvement represents a focused and new way of leading schools to ensure student personalization, decision making, and leadership in their learning.

The concept of an inverted triangle of influence is indeed unique. The traditional hierarchy in education systems typically places those in administrative or policymaking roles at the top. By flipping this hierarchy and placing students and teachers at the top, we are advocating a radical shift in focus onto those who are most directly involved in the learning process. It presents a challenging, but potentially transformative, perspective for school leaders to consider.

Although we advocate that leaders should flip the traditional hierarchy of importance, school leaders must still forge strong relationships with all key external influencers. Flipping the hierarchy means that external stakeholders are key allies and supporters, rather than superiors who scrutinize and judge performance. Building strategic partnerships with people who can provide support, ideas, resources, and endorsement is a task that the school leader should prioritize to create a "willing coalition." Understanding who can block or jeopardize progress is just as important as engaging internally with those who are on your team.

The school leader not only needs to identify the vital external stakeholders who will support and add value to their strategic planning, agency, and ability to "think outside the box," but must also immerse these people in the school community to genuinely allow them to play a part in leading their school for success.

One of our favorite leadership sayings is that great leaders ensure that other people think it was their idea all along! In this role, the leader focuses on developing external partnerships, building alliances, proactively communicating, listening, and responding to the ideas and observations of significant others. Creating and facilitating external influence and support is the key to success for all leaders, but it cannot be simply a strategy; it must be intentional, authentic, and consistent.

As school-empowering leaders become more effective, they become team builders and connectors who bring people together and focus on the collective wisdom of the team. As Michael Fullan (2008) says, it is about allowing the group to improve the group.

IDENTIFY AND BUILD YOUR TRIANGLE OF INFLUENCE

Whether they realize it or not, all schools operate within a triangle of influence; however, it is not always obvious, especially to new leaders, who the external actors are or what level of influence they have on the school and the school leader.

The local triangle of influence starts with those who have an impact on the school at any level. Astute school leaders don't operate in isolation, making decisions and committing resources to initiatives without knowing whether and when there will be positive or negative reactions from anyone (or any organization) that could stifle innovation or school practices. School administrators, government policymakers, school boards, and district-level leaders would immediately come to mind when compiling a hierarchy of influence and importance. Parents and the local community (wider than just those who have children attending the school) are another fundamentally important layer as are school staff, both teaching and nonteaching, who will always have a strong view on all aspects of school operations, whether it is communicated or not. Of course, the key to a hierarchy of influence is the student body, who will convey the success of the school and its leadership through their actions, behavior, and communication, including social media, with parents and community members.

As regular visitors to schools over decades, Jim as a system leader and Yong as an academic, we have had the privilege to engage with a huge number of schools and school leaders and to understand how leaders manage such opportunities to have others enter their school ecosystem. For us, these visits were excellent opportunities to learn about educational issues, innovation, and local schooling as well as understand how high-performing school leaders use their highly developed interpersonal skills to persuade key supporters to become proactive advocates for their school. In some schools, the visits were incredibly well crafted and structured to ensure a mutual transfer of knowledge and core ideas. We talked with the school principals and their leadership teams, visited classes, and often met independently with students and teachers. The teachers seemed to be well-prepared and excited about having guests in their classroom, as were the students.

During other visits, however, we had little time to wander around the school or to randomly talk to people who were not obviously identified by the school leader to engage with us. Though these visits were certainly helpful, we often felt that there was a little too much organization and window dressing. We knew that we were probably being shown the best side of the school, but we often wanted to know more about how the school operated, how teachers felt and thought about their work, and how students experienced the school. This was especially true when schools invited us to engage in conversations about innovation, improvement, and potential change. We felt that we could readily identify which school leaders were seeking to actively engage with us to enhance their school's development and performance and, conversely, which wanted to minimize the risk of us observing aspects of the school that may not have been seen as best practice. After literally hundreds of these interactions, it has become clear to us that there is a large chasm between school leaders who seek to prosper from a hierarchy of influence and those who would rather put a shield around their campus to maintain greater command and control.

School leaders, therefore, have a challenging position in a hierarchy of power and influence in any education system. The "outside world" of the school controls most school resources and also the employment of the school leader. As a result, school leaders must be very aware of the key stakeholders outside their schools, such as legislators, system leaders, policymakers, community leaders, or well-respected academics to benefit from their knowledge, expertise, and observations.

The local and wider media also have enormous influence when issues, both positive and negative, arise within schools or across the profession. Many leaders are very protective and, logically, worried about the outside perceptions of their performance and reputation as leaders. Leaders often try to ensure that the external influencers are satisfied with their performance, which, interestingly, is determined by students, whose experiences are what outsiders always treat as indicators of the quality of schools.

This caution and sensitivity to external influencers, especially to the powers of the education system, drives many school leaders in their work as they try to do what they perceive to be the "right thing." Some leaders, for example, take the outsiders' view of school quality, which is usually manifested in standardized test scores, and thus have become excessively focused on teaching to the test, which is often to the detriment of students and the work of teachers, and results in a lack of commitment to more challenging and personalized curricula. An excessive need to show the system and other outsiders that a school is doing well on standardized tests has, in many cases, resulted in higher numbers of disengaged students and teachers who are afraid to engage students in contemporary learning for fear of not getting the test-related student outcomes required.

Some school leaders feel that they are being judged through a critical lens all the time. Thus, they are constantly considering the expectations of outsiders and work very hard to show that their schools are doing well, to satisfy the outsiders' perspectives. Anxiety about external judgments and concerns can lead school leaders to focus predominantly on external forces instead of the school, the students, and the staff.

Effective school leaders are the gatekeepers. They focus on the priorities. They minimize unwelcome distractions and judgments from the uninformed or disconnected but, as gatekeepers, they do not simply keep the outside world at bay. How leaders choose to represent their schools and open their school environment to the outside world is a key to success. Astute management of school communications and external stakeholder access is a major component of the "new age" school leader. Developing a focused approach to leadership is about controlling the narrative of what your school values and how well it prepares students for an unknown and turbulent future. However, if the school does not offer high-quality education, if the students do not deeply engage and learn meaningfully, and if the teachers and other staff are clearly unhappy, the significant influencers will realize that there is a leadership issue that needs to be addressed. We have seen many cases of schools that have been touted by the school leader as miraculously excellent but, upon deeper exploration, were found to be not nearly as impressive as described.

School leaders are, conversely, in the position to manage outside interference in schools. System leaders, the public, local communities, and outside experts can have all sorts of ideas, policies, requirements, and expectations of how schools should operate. It is the focused school leader who filters these policies and requirements for students and staff in the school. The school leadership team, in conjunction with the teaching staff, needs to collectively interpret system-level policies and external expectations and then implement them to ensure that they are contextually and culturally appropriate. The school leader should not simply adopt external policies, mandates, and expectations of students and staff in the school without assessing whether these potential impositions are fit for purpose in their school and complement current practices and strategy (Kise & Watterston, 2019).

> *The school leadership team, in conjunction with the teaching staff, needs to collectively interpret system-level policies and external expectations and then implement them to ensure that they are contextually and culturally appropriate.*

THE INVERTED TRIANGLE OF INFLUENCE

For school leaders to serve well as the gatekeepers of schools, we invite them to consider a different hierarchy of influence and power where students are at the apex of the triangle of influence (see Figure 2.1). The inverted triangle of influence provides school leaders with a more realistic lens to look at the relationships among the different groups of actors in and outside the education system. It also helps school leaders to consider different relationships, strategic alliances, and ways to build powerful coalitions.

FIGURE 2.1 INVERTING THE TRIANGLE OF INFLUENCE

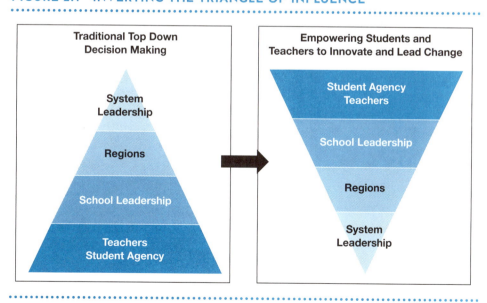

Traditionally, school systems and schools operate based on positional power. That is, the system leaders sit at the apex of the pyramid, and their decisions cascade down to external regional leaders and influencers, school leaders, the community, and teachers and students. In this traditional pyramid, teachers lack agency as policies, programs, and mandates trickle down to the classrooms where teachers must faithfully implement them.

> *The inverted triangle of influence provides school leaders with a more realistic lens to look at the relationships among the different groups of actors in and outside the education system. It also helps school leaders to consider different relationships, strategic alliances, and ways to build powerful coalitions.*

To empower students to have agency over their learning, we are advocating that leaders invert the notional triangle of influence to ensure that students and teachers become the prime focus of team-driven strategy and leadership, while leaders and influencers move to the lower end of the pyramid. This conceptual model is important as a representation to your community of who and what is valued across your school ecosystem. An inverted pyramid of influence also aligns significant others to focus on contextual school development, progress, and performance, as opposed to the traditional model of line management in which teachers and school leaders are subservient to external leaders and influencers.

In the inverted triangle of influence, we place students at the top as they are the reasons schools exist. Unless students are well served, no school can be considered successful. As Figure 2.1 displays, customers (students) always come first, as every action taken must be focused on improving engagement and performance.

Next in the hierarchy of influence and importance are well-supported and highly valued teachers, who provide direct services, care, support, and guidance to students. In most traditional education systems, however, teachers are placed above students because they facilitate and support everything that matters in students' learning experiences. They diligently plan what is learned, how is it learned, when is it learned, and how learning is judged. It is imperative that teachers are the drivers of contemporary learning and not simply the implementers of mandated curricula. School leaders must clearly demonstrate to teachers that their importance is built on students' agency and engagement.

During the COVID-19 pandemic, teachers across the world demonstrated their capacity for innovation and their deep care for their students as students learned remotely without any previous experience or blueprints on how this could be managed. These actions confirmed that the real architects of positive change are those in classrooms who know what each student needs despite their uniqueness and challenges. The inverted triangle of influence places teachers along with students at the top of school success, and it is the aim of the school leader to ensure that each teacher is supported to be the best they can be.

Districts, regional offices, bureaucracies, and other external influencers have traditionally been considered above schools in terms of governance, direction, and oversight; however, in terms of direct influence and implementation, they are below teachers. All external elements of the education system provide services to schools and monitor the quality of education schools provide. They are important, but in terms of the impact on students, not nearly as influential as teachers. They enable and support teachers rather than exercising control or oversight.

Educational systems leaders, policymakers, assessment administrators, and government agencies are placed at the lower part of the inverted triangle. This is not to say that they are not important, but their relevance is to ensure schools are properly run, students are safe and protected, and teachers are well supported. School leaders should treat this layer of players and practices as the most basic guarantee for students and schools. Although compliance with system and regional policies is required, in a business sense, system leaders are the commissioners of school performance and outcomes, thereby giving the school license to ensure achievement.

SERVE THE STUDENTS, NOT THE SYSTEM

How should school principals align and implement this inverted triangle of influencers to ensure that the locus of control remains with those working in classrooms? The highest imperative is to align everyone in the education system to serve teachers and their students instead of serving the system. In other words, school leaders, no matter what they do, should work to benefit students.

If students are indeed to be considered the most powerful and important people in the school, then it is the role of school leaders to engage with all stakeholders to ensure that the school culture has students at the center. Students are the customers and customers anywhere hold the most important position in judging the quality of an organization or institution.

The quality of a school ultimately must be experienced and reported by students or indicated by the development of their abilities, the cultivation of their passions, and the fostering of their values and personalities. The quality is also indicated by their standardized achievement scores.

However, like customers in a restaurant, students themselves have the power to decide if their school experiences are engaging and meaningful. Restaurants prepare and offer food, services, drinks, and appealing settings to customers, but they are unable to dictate how customers feel about their experiences. Ultimately, it is the customers who decide what they think of the restaurants. The power rests with the customers. This is the same for students and their parents and caregivers, who possess the power to decide whether their school experiences are of sufficient quality to meet their expectations.

Different from restaurant customers, students participate in a school experience for years, and it obviously has a lot more impact. If a customer has a bad experience in a restaurant, the impact is very small. But if a student has a bad experience in school, the experience has a lasting effect that can influence social and emotional conditions, personality, cognitive development, and ethical and moral development. School experience directly affects the student's life in the school and in the future as well.

We are depending on future generations of students to be the potential leaders and problem-solvers of the world. Thus the mindsets, ethics, moral standards, and abilities they develop determine how the existential challenges might be met and what the future world will be. The degree to which our students grow up to become responsible, compassionate, innovative, and capable citizens will largely decide the effects and impact of technological advancement, human conflicts, climate change, cultural acceptance, and potential global pandemics. Students, after all, are not being prepared for the future, but to create the future.

Therefore, highly effective school leaders must empower their teaching team to nurture and support each and every student inclusively as a unique and important member of a collaborative and connected community. Treating students as the most important and powerful group in school is easier said than done because students are not traditionally given agency or influence over how schools operate. Thus, developing a hierarchy of importance in your school with students at the apex requires school leaders to enable students to develop and embrace that ownership.

Suggested Action Steps for Supporting Students

Create a Culture That Empowers Students

Successful school leaders work with teachers and other stakeholders to make clear that students are important and powerful. Although the message may have been delivered before and the adults in the school may already understand and believe it, the school leader must work with staff to identify specific strategies to place all students at the center of the school. Students could influence the school timetable, staff selection processes, class organization, curriculum, assessment, homework, student organizations, and other aspects of the school experience. It is central to engagement that students work with teachers to influence decisions that affect them and their learning (Hattie, 2023). In general, such discussions do not happen very often as staff are usually more focused on what to teach instead of who they are teaching.

Give Students Time

Students need their own time to develop ownership of their learning. School leaders need to work on a strategy with all staff to create more time for students to work on what matters to them. It is no secret that we overteach in schools, which was confirmed by remote learning during the COVID-19 pandemic.

For students to be the owners of their learning (Zhao, 2012), they need more control of their time and the ability to exercise their right of self-determination (Wehmeyer & Zhao, 2020); in other words, they require flexibility and decision-making capacity from teachers to personalize their learning. Schools have traditionally not been able to give students control of time; thus, we must work with teachers to free students so that they are able to create their own learning experiences (Watterston & Zhao, 2023).

Invite Students to Own Their Learning

School leaders need to work with students to make sure that they understand they are important, respected, and agents of change in the school (Kise & Watterston, 2019). Asking students to assume ownership of learning is quite challenging because most have never been provided with an opportunity to practice how to own their learning and how to exercise their influence and choices. Owning one's learning means the person must have sufficient empowerment to make these decisions while taking responsibility. Instead of relying on or being controlled by teachers or schools, students should be encouraged to pursue their interests, comply with a small set of requirements, and explore in teams and on their own. This requires the entire school to change its culture to place the students at the center. Implement policies and practices that enable students to exercise their voices, contribute their ideas and expertise, and bear responsibility for their actions.

Help Students Develop Capacity

Finally, school leaders should work on helping students develop their ability to exert agency in their learning. First, students need to develop the psychological capacity to own their learning (Hattie, 2023). In traditional schools, students sit in the classroom, listen to the teacher, and complete required work. They do not always have to think about why they are learning, what they are learning, or how to make learning serve their purposes. Implement programs or courses that help students navigate how to take responsibility and how to manage their own learning.

EMPOWER AND TRUST TEACHERS TO MAKE IMPORTANT DECISIONS

The primary focus of highly effective leaders is to provide students with a high-quality learning experience (Robinson et al., 2017). Effective leaders understand that a high-quality learning experience is only possible when teachers and other staff share the same goals and aspirations for their students (Leithwood et al., 2017). They are aware that the entire school needs to be involved in creating high-quality learning environments, and it is impossible for the school leader alone to do so.

> *Effective leaders understand that a high-quality learning experience is only possible when teachers and other staff share the same goals and aspirations for their students. They are aware that the entire school needs to be involved in creating high-quality learning environments, and it is impossible for the school leader alone to do so.*

Suggested Action Steps for Empowering Teachers

Empower Teachers as Key Agents for Change

School leaders are usually accustomed to initiating change and working with staff on the implementation. Our experience during the COVID-19 pandemic, however, has underscored the benefits of teachers collectively leading change based on their knowledge and understanding of their students. It is incumbent upon school leaders to provide resources, time, and support to enable teachers to become architects of improved pedagogical practices and engaging curricula. School leaders need to provide opportunities for staff to work in teams and with experts to adjust and reform current programs and courses to ensure better performance and outcomes. Great leaders facilitate these opportunities to enable teacher growth and leadership and to address identified problems of practice. Developing a culture of teacher-led evidence-based improvement and innovation stimulates classroom teachers as they build their collective understanding of what works and under what conditions. It is a culture of learning that demonstrates to students that we are all lifelong learners. Through conversations with teachers about their work, the leader prompts and guides them into more challenging investigations and interventions, which provides great responsibility and accountability to build their agency and an improvement agenda. School leaders work on developing and inspiring teachers to make changes by wanting to know what they do instead of telling them what they should do.

Grow Innovative Leaders

Growing teachers into creative innovation leaders is the ultimate legacy a school leader should work on. No matter how long the tenure is, school leaders eventually leave the school. What is left behind after their departure? It is the people who have grown cognitively, psychologically, and socially. A great leader always creates an environment that empowers and inspires others to grow, democratizes leadership, and draws on teachers to lead innovation. If your staff members become school leaders in other schools or develop innovative educational programs, you can consider yourself to have been a high-performing leader who has contributed to future-proofing education practice as new leaders emerge with a forward-facing focus instead of reverting to past practices.

*Acknowledge Teachers' Contributions and **Achievements***

Great leaders know and acknowledge the contributions and significant achievements of teachers and other staff. While always inspiring staff to achieve and innovate more, high-performing leaders also set the expectations for excellence, innovation, and personalization for the entire school community. Innovative teachers and staff are recognized in newsletters, on social media, and in other media and events. For example, schools can hold annual or semi-annual innovation days when teachers are recognized for their achievements and share their excellent work with students, the school community, and top leaders as well as other outsiders.

PARTNER WITH DISTRICT AND REGIONAL OFFICES

District and regional offices traditionally operate above the school leader and the school. They liaise and, at times, direct the school principal and monitor the performance of the school on behalf of the education system and taxpayers. In many ways, school leaders influence and have oversight from these offices, which deliver policies, practice guidelines, assessment requirements, curriculum interpretations, performance reviews, and enforce regulations from the education system. These offices may also develop and provide professional development, technological resources, library and media resources, services for special education students as well as for gifted and talented programs, and other services related to finance and employment.

These offices are designed as the enabler of education offered in schools. They hold school leaders accountable to ensure that high-quality education happens in all schools; however, their interpretation of high-quality education may deviate from that of the school leader and staff in schools. It is likely that these offices will focus on limited measures of achievement such as test scores, instead of the broader range of skills and knowledge provided in schools.

It is, therefore, a prime responsibility of high-performing school leaders to actively develop proactive relationships with these external leaders to ensure that there is awareness, and understanding, of your school's strategy, values, culture, priorities, achievements, and challenges, so that they can support your school's practices and evidence-based innovations. Inviting key leaders to regularly visit and interact with your school and community to observe quality teaching and learning serves their interests, and for staff, the visits will eliminate the mystique surrounding "those who watch over them." Seeking advice and learning from their observations of your school builds a willing coalition as expertise is shared and supported.

Highly effective school leaders make optimal use of these offices. Rarely do they engage in conflict with them, even when they may have differing perceptions of best practices or other issues. When differences appear, it is important for the credible school leader to understand and support that these offices often must implement policies and regulations that have been made by policymakers. Smart leaders always work with these offices to seek compromise or solutions instead of building a barrier or dismissing them.

Suggested Action Steps for Partnering With District and Regional Offices

Present Your School's Successes and Struggles Honestly

Effective leaders always present a clear and authentic picture of the school to the office, so they understand the opportunities and challenges facing the school leader. School leaders should invite representatives, superintendents, or other leaders from these offices to regularly visit their schools and to attend and participate in school events. They should also, whenever possible, speak with relevant leaders about their actions in schools such as innovative pedagogies, courses, and exceptional teachers and students. The notion is to give the office a clear understanding that the school is always learning, making progress, reforming, and innovating through the leader empowering those who teach and deliver services across the school.

Use District Resources Effectively

Effective school leaders are also very good at actively advocating for targeted resources and support from the school district, central offices, and regional offices, grounded in evidence-based strategy formulation. Although the specific resources each district or regional office provides vary, smart school leaders are very aware of the available resources and work hard to get them for their schools. They are accountable for all resourcing and collect relevant and valuable data to demonstrate progress and innovation, which can be shared with other schools. They are always considering the needs of their students, with empowered teachers initiating enhanced ways to help students and colleagues improve practice, outcomes, and engagement. Moreover, high-performing leaders are always looking to inform students and teachers of new and experimental funding opportunities from diverse sources, including the central or regional office.

Share Innovation Successes With the Central Office

Effective school leaders share noteworthy innovations and success at their school sites with regional and central office leaders. District offices are always on the lookout for successful strategies that they can share at other school sites. Make a practice of promoting the exemplary work of teachers and the amazing achievements of your students. The district leaders will share these stories and cite them as evidence of change and credibility. Build meaningful alliances with other schools to create coalitions that develop and share best practices for the benefit of all. Great leaders and high-performing schools are not in competition; they learn from their colleagues and ensure that everyone succeeds.

Drive and provide constructive feedback regarding the central and regional office's services to make sure that they work for the school and serve the most important elements of schools—students and teachers.

> *Drive and provide constructive feedback regarding the central and regional office's services to make sure that they work for the school and serve the most important elements of schools–students and teachers.*

EDUCATION SYSTEM BUREAUCRACY AND POLICYMAKERS

At the base of the inverted triangle are the top-level bureaucracy and policymakers. This can be a large body of institutions such as national or state curriculum authorities, examination boards, education boards, state or national department/ministry of education, and various authorities of credentialing or accreditation. These high-level institutions are traditionally at the top of the education hierarchy because they make policies and practice guidelines or frameworks for the entire education system. They also make decisions about funding formulae and dispense funding to all schools.

These jurisdictional institutions are powerful, but their impact is delivered indirectly through curriculum standards, standardized test results, funding policies and formulae, or other requirements such as pedagogical approaches. School leaders flexibly manage these policies and regulations to contextualize and structure the impact on the school, ensuring compliance and added value.

Although it is possible for school leaders to raise issues and voice opposition to certain policies and regulations, policy-level changes usually take a long time to be enacted. Smart and informed school leaders raise key questions, seek to understand, and propose school-based implementation plans that proactively absorb policies.

OTHER ACTORS IN THE TRIANGLE OF INFLUENCE

The local community around your school is also a key and important player in the education system. Local residents have a great interest in the quality and test scores of local schools, not only because they affect real estate prices. Publishers of textbooks and teaching materials also have a strong interest in, and an impact on, schools as they seek to support teaching and learning. Educational researchers and universities can impact schools through their research translation and school development programs, as well as external programs that support career paths for school administrators. Local media have an impact as does the social media behavior of teachers, students, parents, and school leaders.

All these actors and players, though not listed in the inverted triangle, are enablers and potential supporters or distractors of your school's performance. School leaders can harness them as supporters and enablers.

- Develop ways to reach out to let them know what your school is doing.

- Inform them of teacher innovations and student activities.

- Host evening or weekend events that are open to the public.

- Utilize social media to reach a broad community beyond the school.

- Disseminate publications for parents.

- Share your innovations and learning practices widely to enable all actors across all parts of the inverted triangle to promote and share your evidence-based learnings.

When well informed, these actors can help the school to realize its visions and provide resources that serve the purpose of the school.

CHAPTER 2 FOCUS POINTS

1. Students in high-performing schools are clearly at the apex: The inverted triangle illustrates that the ultimate beneficiaries of the education system—students—should be at the top of the hierarchy. School leaders must prioritize the needs, aspirations, and holistic development of students when making strategic decisions.

2. Teachers' role: Teachers play a critical role as direct facilitators of student learning. Recognizing their importance reinforces that teachers are not merely implementers of dictated curricula but should be empowered to innovate and tailor learning experiences based on the unique needs of their students. School leaders should, therefore, focus on providing teachers with the necessary support and resources, valuing their expertise, and promoting their autonomy.

3. External influencers: External stakeholders, such as regional or district offices and community influencers, fall below teachers in the inverted triangle. Their primary role is to provide support services to schools and ensure quality education. Although their influence is less direct than that of teachers, their input and support remain crucial for the smooth functioning of schools.

4. System and policymakers: At the base of the triangle are system leaders, policymakers, and government agencies. They provide the foundational structures and safeguards within which schools operate. Although they do not always interact with students directly, they play a significant role in setting the broader education agenda and providing necessary resources.

CHAPTER 3

····································

LEADING TO CREATE A GAME PLAN FOR SUCCESS

Focusing on a Game Plan for Success

Quite a few years ago, Jim, as the principal of a very large K–7 elementary school, was somewhat surprised when one of the more than 100 teachers present at an after-school staff meeting asked why he (Jim) tolerated teachers who raised their voices or yelled at students. Jim was shocked by the question and immediately responded that he didn't believe that anyone should ever yell at a student, no matter what the justification might be. An hour-long debate ensued as teachers passionately proposed reasons why raising their voices would be appropriate in certain circumstances while many others countered that they did not ever want colleagues raising their voices when dealing with students.

Jim initially worried such a challenging and emotional discussion was overtaking the meeting agenda, but it quickly became clear that this was a pivotal moment in his leadership journey, and it was the catalyst for much longer-term cultural reform to build a stronger and more collaborative staff team. Instead of this debate dividing the room and highlighting differences of opinion, it was a light-bulb moment when he realized the school needed a game plan that united staff and made clear "how we all collectively do things here." It needed to be a game plan that bonded staff together around shared values and consistency of practice without creating mandates that would erode the uniqueness and passions of individuals. The school game plan proved to be a pivotal "playbook" that created teacher agency and agreement about the way things got done to optimize outcomes and the student experience.

This chapter focuses on why culture and alignment are so important to success in any endeavor and how this is proactively and positively developed in an educational setting based on the values and practices that are prioritized by the organization. The best-organized enterprises will fail without a collaborative, aligned, and supportive culture whose whole is much greater than the sum of its parts. Focused school leaders build and sustain an inclusive, professional, and supportive culture that enables everyone to succeed in a learning community. The ultimate determination of satisfaction and success for any group of people, be it a family, political party, or school, is the quality of its team-based culture.

Progressive and high-performing school principals improve school performance by systematically improving school culture (Hattie, 2015). School improvement does not occur by mandate. It is impossible to improve performance without high-quality staff leading collaboratively. Too often, the latest formula for systemwide improvement is politically and administratively devised and those in classrooms are then required to faithfully implement the new strategies and directives, often without any agency or validation.

School leaders and teachers often introduce new strategic priorities, but they don't always consider the context, culture, and capability of individual schools and systems when making those changes. School improvement is not just about new strategic directions; it is just as much about ownership, engagement, and, most important, the development and implementation of a game plan that contributes to a consistent and dependable culture for improvement.

As the chapter's opening vignette illustrates, there is a more empowering and aligned way of generating systemic and school-site improvement. It requires the establishment of a democratic culture that will open the door to locally driven improved school performance and quality educational practice. Although not everyone in the education profession warms to sporting analogies, the notion of a school producing a team game plan, from our experience, can proactively harmonize the school culture and practices by aligning staff and creating agency for all.

Every elite team has a unique and customized game plan that guides strategy, the way they play, how they behave, how they train, how they treat and value their fans, and how they want to be perceived as an organization. They aim to be inclusive and connected to their fans and stakeholders by providing proactive communication, loyalty, and a great experience for all followers. Although you may not want to call your school operating model a "game plan," it is evident to us that great schools should engage with their stakeholders to ensure strategic agreement and consistency.

When sporting teams do not experience success, fans often become agitated and want to see changes made, along with evidence that better times are coming. At these times, focused communication is imperative as the team provides regular updates about its renewal, recruitment, and strategic changes to the game plan, and to ensure that stakeholders feel they are part of the solution, with the knowledge that the club is working hard to remedy the situation. Sharing adjustments and a reset to the game plan is what fans expect and welcome to give them hope. Schools are certainly not elite sporting teams, but creating a focused and transparent plan is essential to maintaining stakeholder support through listening, connection, inclusion, and positive participation.

Employing a sporting analogy as an approach to school improvement may be useful, but it does not work when it comes to competition between schools. In the sporting world, teams measure themselves on finishing above other teams and improving their performance by surprising their opposition with unique and secret plays to gain an advantage. But in the field of education, treating other schools and systems as the opposition negatively impacts everyone involved. Ideally, schools share their trade secrets of success as much as possible, ensuring that all schools improve and exceed expectations.

Unfortunately, competition does exist within the wider education ecosystem. Much of this competitiveness stems from national testing and high-stakes ranking in which schools vie for enrolments and reputation. The culture of competitiveness among schools is weakening our capacity to reduce the equity gap between high and low socioeconomic areas. A successful school leader focuses on sharing what works and contributes to building best practices across the whole ecosystem.

For decades we have engaged with many individual schools who continue to focus on reinventing the wheel while there are much better "wheels" at the school just down the road. We owe it to every student and their families, no matter where they live, to make sure that *every great school has a great school down the road*. A child's zip code cannot be the determinant of her or his educational success and consequent life chances. An effective starting point is building a culture in which schools—whether public, charter, private, or parochial—are empowered to learn from each other rather than isolating themselves due to a misguided notion that they are in cut-throat competition with each other. Even within the public system, schools compete to build numbers and reputation at the expense of neighboring public schools. There is no point starting from scratch, wasting much-needed energy and resources, if another school can show you the way and save you time and effort.

In many parts of the world, education is suffering from an unwillingness of many to share and work with each other across jurisdictional boundaries to ensure every school is brilliant. Imagine hospitals keeping new medical procedures a secret to ensure that cutting-edge treatment could only be accessed at a single location so as to attract patients away from other hospitals. This is often the case across the education landscape between schools, systems, and even states and countries.

We can do better. For that to happen, school leaders must promote a game plan that is structured on sharing practice and innovation with other like-minded

> *Promote a game plan that is structured on sharing practice and innovation with other likeminded schools. . . . We have witnessed wonderful but isolated examples in some cities and towns where clusters of schools from different sectors are working together with great effect and with no loss of existing market share.*

schools. We need to leverage expertise and successful experiences so that all students can succeed. We have witnessed wonderful but isolated examples in some cities and towns where clusters of schools from different sectors are working together with great effect and with no loss of existing market share. This needs to be the norm, not the exception.

For schools to work together in a less competitive environment, school leaders need the know-how to empower staff to take the lead and build a culture that ensures every teacher is working as part of a sharing, high-performing team. Leadership know-how is best achieved by less talking and more listening, observing, doing, and questioning.

LEADING A UNIQUE SCHOOL GAME PLAN

John Dewey, in his seminal book, *Democracy and Education* (1916), aligns with the aspiration of this book, which is about being able to make progressive and contemporary changes to the organization and delivery of education to suit the times. He states,

> Particularly it is true that a society which not only changes but which has the ideal of such change as will improve it, will have different standards and methods of education from one which aims simply at the perpetuation of its own customs. (p. 81)

Almost every school has a strategic plan of some sort. Such a plan commonly identifies priorities, required resources, what needs to be done, and by whom. Quite often, however, time-limited strategic plans do not tell the whole story of what is culturally and procedurally important to teachers, and often not everyone in the school is directly connected to the priorities identified. For any plan to bear fruit, all staff need to be able to "see" themselves and identify their work as a pivotal base for the plan to be successfully delivered. A game plan is, however, a more comprehensive vehicle than just a strategic plan. A game plan goes much further in reforming and articulating classroom practices to stakeholders, identifying agreed behavior management practices, well-being, pedagogy, curricula, special needs, assessment, concerns, students, parents, and many other key elements of school performance.

A school game plan is always evolving with the inclusion of additional policies, agreements, and revisions of redundant practices or new requirements. Importantly however, the game plan becomes a macro version of the school's business card as it provides a window for external stakeholders to see into, and understand, the school practices, so it must be authentic and collaboratively implemented and owned by all staff so that external stakeholders feel confident and have a part to play in the success of the school.

One way of connecting external and internal stakeholders is to become more transparent and inclusive about how the school develops and monitors the organization's shared beliefs, values, processes, practices, and priorities, with an aim to build a willing coalition across the wider community. John P. Kotter (1999), in his book *What Leaders Really Do*, identifies a range of errors that leaders make when transformation efforts fail. He identifies that "not building a powerful enough guiding coalition" significantly limits the potential for sustained organizational success.

Building an inclusive learning community in which agency and contribution are openly invited and recognized enables the school leader to become a connector and facilitator of a game plan built on agreement, as opposed to simply managing disagreement between staff and the wider community. Building the density of leadership and creating transparency across a learning community does not lessen the influence and significance of the appointed leader; on the contrary, we have regularly observed that building and supporting collaborative teams creates greater leverage and impact for the school leader as the team proactively contributes to improving practice.

A recent social media post noted that an important pathway to leading a happy life is to become much harder to offend. Becoming much harder to offend is, indeed, a most important trait for a school leader. Being harder to offend is about proactively sharing accountability for the game plan and school performance with the team and not taking criticism personally. Staying positive and treating adversities as an opportunity to refine or better explain "how we do things around here" requires a successful game plan that stakeholders can continue to influence.

We have met many high-performing school leaders who have transitioned from Lone Ranger leaders to sheepdog leaders who are constantly moving around and vigilantly observing to protect the flock. Sheepdogs rarely lead from the front, hoping that the sheep just follow; instead, they regularly move to the back, the side, or the middle of the flock while at times circling and intervening as they look out for impediments and danger. For sheepdogs, the aim is to calm the flock, making sure that everyone is protected and that they work together and safely reach their destination. Although school principals do a lot more than just protect their "flock," the analogy of being in the right place at the right time is a fundamental characteristic of high-performing leaders.

Based on our extensive experience and observation of many school leaders, we have identified common attributes of focused and high-performing leaders who are prepared to empower teams to bring about change through innovation and collaborative practices.

Game Plan Leaders Are . . .

- **Trustworthy.** They authentically build trust with all stakeholders.

- **Inclusive.** They believe that everyone is important to the team.

- **Humble.** They lead with humility and pass the pronoun test (we, us, and our instead of me, my, and I).

- **Empathic.** They proactively support staff to prioritize adverse personal events over their work during stressful times.

- **Forgiving.** They believe that everyone deserves multiple chances and support to overcome obstacles and that mistakes are opportunities for personal and professional growth

- **Empowering.** They mentor, support, and coach to build up new leaders.

- **Build Sustainability.** Their legacy to the school upon departure is the quality of leadership they leave behind to maintain the momentum to move the school forward.

In short, school leaders do not need to do everything in their school. Their job is to protect and support the whole team to reach their destination safely while enjoying the journey.

THE GAME PLAN: DEMOCRATIZING THE "WAY WE DO THINGS AROUND HERE"

Jim's story at the beginning of this chapter described a real-life example of teachers in the same school having very different views on how students experienced behavior management in their classrooms. Teachers clearly identified that they had very different approaches to how they dealt with students, but the debate at the staff meeting was concluded by putting together a small task force of committed teachers to further consult with stakeholders to create a draft student management policy and eventually a statement that was shared with the community.

Every teacher in the school was asked to contribute to this process, at the very least, by reviewing the policy and ensuring that it was acceptable from their perspective. This process took many months and many edits to get to the point of publishing. Even then, it was reviewed on a regular basis over the next few years as new practices and ideas emerged regarding the behavior management of students. What started as a debate about teachers raising their voices in the classroom resulted in a powerful and inclusive policy and a change in school culture.

During this pivotal time in his career, Jim grew in his understanding that leading a school did not mean that he was obligated to do all the heavy lifting on his own. The democratization of decision making was applied to every important issue brought to the table by teachers, community stakeholders, and school leaders embracing a consensus decision-making approach. For a time, decision making and resolution took much longer as staff debated and researched new initiatives, policy positions, and programs, but as each issue was resolved, staff engagement and teacher agency continued to solidify.

> *For a time, decision making and resolution took much longer as staff debated and researched new initiatives, policy positions, and programs, but as each issue was resolved, staff engagement and teacher agency continued to solidify.*

The idea of developing new or revised school, teacher, and student policies and practices into a school game plan was a natural extension of a more collaborative culture in which those who were delivering services in classrooms became the architects of what was contextually appropriate and best practice. Over time, debates quickly became solution focused and compromise was reached more quickly as an integrated planning process reflected the expectation that "we are all in this together."

CREATING TIME AND SPACE FOR INNOVATION AND REFORM

Creating a game plan requires resources and time to enable staff to work in teams to address problems of practice and research new initiatives. Teachers are already time poor, so providing agency in decision making requires time release to work on the game plan. The role of school leaders is to prioritize resources to release teachers to enable them to apply themselves to the task at hand. In our turbulent and rapidly changing world, schools cannot wait for governments or school systems to provide policies or top-down mandates about new technologies, community expectations, contemporary curricula imperatives, enhanced pedagogical practices, well-being, and student re-engagement demands. Schools need to be on the front foot as local and global priorities emerge so as not to leave students preparing for a life that requires different competencies, skills, and knowledge. Focused leaders make focused decisions to ensure that students are operating at the cusp of innovation and discovery. Students need to be the problem solvers of tomorrow, so they don't need to be trapped in our thinking from decades past.

During the COVID-19 pandemic, in the schools where lockdowns persisted for longer periods of time, teachers experienced burnout due to overwhelming workloads and the accompanying stress. One strategy to alleviate that stress in some schools was to provide substitute teachers—giving teachers both much-needed rest and the gift of time to access expertise by researching improved practices that might lessen their workload.

WORKING IN TEAMS

The applied science of team building is an absolute necessity for any organization to be successful. In her article "Teaching Is a Team Sport," Cooper (2017) reminds us that teachers working together to collaborate and share ideas, solutions, and differing expertise recognize the benefits that students gain from collaborating during group work. Teachers can reap benefits from working together to reduce personal workloads, improve practice, and collectively achieve better outcomes. Teams, however, don't just naturally emerge, especially in large education departments and systems. In education, team building is a highly complex science that shapes the culture and determines the ultimate success of the organization. Teams need to be united by professional, personal, and moral agreement about "how we get things done around here." Obtaining the buy-in of others is highly challenging work.

High-quality teaching and focused school leadership are almost impossible without an agreed game plan that engages everyone and to which there is willing adherence and accountability (Australian Institute for Teaching and School Leadership [AITSL], 2016). Positional power can get subordinates to comply and meet most deadlines, at least in times of crisis. It is, however, not a long-term strategy because it does not always engender longer-term commitment or loyalty. If a leader relies on positional power, over time they don't really have any power at all. The art of creating a narrative for change and engaging people in constructing and supporting that change is through the authentic empowerment of others. Tapping into the experience, enthusiasm, and skills of others creates excitement, boosts esteem, and builds morale.

Getting mid-level and senior-level leaders to change their leadership practices is often a formidable challenge. Language, tone, and gestures are very powerful and influence workplace cultures both positively and negatively. A leader's anxiety, high expectations, and ongoing catastrophizing often reinforce the power imbalance and increase the fear of failure for subordinates. To build sustainable teams, leaders need to invest time in supporting and mentoring colleagues while sharing successes and challenges with the group. Such a team-oriented culture is founded on asking "How can I help?" as opposed to "Here's what I need you to do."

Culture change must be modeled from the top through constant dialogue and consistent review of practice and interactions to confirm expected behaviors. Consistency is then enhanced by collective reflection and ongoing dialogue. A key role in ensuring positive and sustained cultural change is to keep checking with all staff team members at regular meetings and, importantly, to consistently circulate across all classrooms to better understand the challenges and success that all teachers face. Leaders regularly assess whether the rhetoric matches reality and check in to see if the culture is authentic or contrived. This can be done by collecting teacher and leader data through annual surveys, but also by constantly observing and listening to issues and discussing how well, as a team, a proactive and connected culture is adding value to their work. One strategy that has worked well for Jim has been a group dialogue he calls "The Captain's Table."

Invite People to the Captain's Table

As a 21-year-old, Jim once took a cruise with some friends. One night he unexpectedly received a single invitation to the Captain's Table for dinner. He discovered that the captain genuinely wanted to know from his randomly selected guests what they thought of the cruise so far. The captain listened intently and then asked what he and the crew could do better. It wasn't an idle question because a few days later, the captain checked in with each of his dinner guests to see if they had noticed any changes.

Many years later, as a first-time school principal, Jim found that convening similar meetings to check in with randomly selected staff at all levels was a wonderful way to take the team's pulse and discuss the culture. Meetings usually started slowly, but once participants were relaxed, conversations and feedback became forthright, candid, and proactive.

LEVERAGING THE GAME PLAN TO LEAD THE CAPABILITY BUILDING OF STAFF

When it comes to the implementation of individual performance development of all staff, the school's game plan is a pivotal platform upon which staff members can be coached, supported, and proactively accountable. A game plan that contains stakeholder-generated agreements, positive actions, and policies provides clear and collaborative goals for performance monitoring. Ensure that all members of the team are committed to the game plan and provide support, professional development, and peer coaching so that collaboration and quality teaching can drive the school's performance.

In many schools, leaders regularly tell us that managing the performance of individual school staff is an onerous expectation that, despite great intentions, often falls by the wayside due to escalating time pressures as the school year progresses. Instead of the traditional one-on-one performance review, ask staff to reflect upon the game plan and identify personal collaborative priorities to enhance practices in teams. This will not only be more productive and efficient, but it can boost the school culture as agreement is built around the "way we do things" at our school.

Recruiting new staff is also both a significant challenge and a great opportunity. It is challenging because the wrong choice could negatively impact the culture, trust, and team-based orientation of the school, but conversely, it is also an opportunity to enhance the team and bring new ideas to "how we do things around here." The school's game plan should be a very important component of the appointment process for new staff, and it could well make candidate selection easier.

Send your school's game plan to all candidates as part of the job description. This will immediately alert applicants that there is a unified way that your school does things, and unless they are comfortable and excited about aligning with your school's game plan, they should probably join another team.

In order to select a team player who will add value to your work, use the game plan during the interview to gauge applicants' understanding of the agreements and beliefs that underpin your school. The game plan is also an integral component of a comprehensive induction process for new staff. Talking with teaching staff and understanding the school's culture, values, and opportunities will also increase the confidence and commitment of new team members.

In addition to a game plan approach to recruiting new staff, one of the key roles that focused school leaders undertake is to proactively "re-recruit" disengaged staff who are already teaching at the school. Whenever we have met school leaders to discuss their work and how they focus on improving student outcomes, just about every leader says something along the lines of "If only those three staff who are just going through the motions and resisting being a part of the team could be more positive and connected, we would all be a lot better off. They distract new teachers and speak negatively about our school to external stakeholders, which limits our stakeholder relationships."

For a multitude of reasons, such as personal conflicts, disagreement about strategy, feeling ignored or not consulted, or feeling unappreciated, disengaged staff can and do impact heavily on the school's culture and progress. Negativity spreads and divides teams and inhibits momentum, so these disaffected staff should not be left to their own devices. Poorly performing teachers are not a leader's problem: They are very much an opportunity. Teams are only as good as their weakest link, so it is imperative that those outliers are re-recruited into the team structure. This is not an easy assignment because these teachers have often felt isolated and poorly treated for a long time; turning them around requires deep understanding, authentic opportunities to contribute, and support to rebuild relationships. It's important to provide people with an opportunity to engage and participate in customized professional development, and to recognize their strengths instead of focusing on their flaws, but engaging them in healthy game plan debates and working groups so they have some agency is the beginning of the pathway to inclusion.

Rarely does anyone come to work with the intention to do harm, so finding ways to recognize and support their work is a first step toward creating a proactive team member who is collectively designing "the way we do things around here." Leaders must remember that every single one of us has a back story, and once this is better known and appreciated, there is at least a chance to rebuild trust and commitment. Many people do not share challenging problems, such as health disorders, domestic violence, mental health concerns, economic issues, and so on. Everyone's story is different, so finding the key and understanding the person comes well before dealing with the work's shortcomings. Although school leaders are not psychiatrists, and nor should they try to be, building authentic relationships with all members of the team is the first step. Engage professionals to support your staff, and appreciate that their work behavior is undoubtedly driven by a myriad of external and internal issues that cannot always be managed by the individual concerned. As a leader, there is no better reward than supporting a colleague to focus on their job after they have been able to deal with the issues that were preventing their full engagement.

Another great strategy is to set up a Leadership Collective consisting of all of those in teaching and nonteaching leadership roles. The Leadership Collective meets regularly (twice a month or monthly) to reflect and learn as a team about impactful leadership and teamwork. Standing agenda items for this group include sharing problems of practice: Leaders detail issues that may or may not have gone smoothly. Our experience is that sharing examples with the collective builds trust. Questions such as "What else could you have done?" and "Who did you consult with before making that decision?" can be probed further so that the whole group learns from their colleagues' experience and decision making. Leadership Collective members can also provide regular reports in which they share progress with the collective to ensure that all leadership portfolio strategic initiatives are visible and aligned.

> *Sharing examples with the collective builds trust. Questions such as "What else could you have done?" and "Who did you consult with before making that decision?" can be probed further so that the whole group learns from their colleagues' experience and decision making.*

It is also useful to bring in external leaders to provide professional development and discuss new ideas. Invite senior external leaders—systems leaders, local politicians, leaders of media organizations, technology icons, and others in professions that impact education—to meet with the Leadership Collective. These interactions provide collective members with greater confidence and an opportunity to form relationships with key leaders who may mentor them or even provide opportunities to be placed in other organizations to build their leadership understandings and capabilities.

It is hard to provide a comprehensive list of the high-level elements that can be included in the game plan, as the point is to capture unique issues and problems of practice. But in the main, the following themes provide a structure for game plan development.

CHAPTER 3 • LEADING TO CREATE A GAME PLAN FOR SUCCESS 51

SUGGESTED ELEMENTS TO INCLUDE IN STRONG GAME PLANS

- **Codes of conduct for staff, students, and stakeholders.** What standards do we expect and how do we deal with behavior management and breaches of the codes? What do we expect from each other? How and when do we identify the need for a review of any part of the game plan?

- **Mission statement.** What is the purpose of our school in a turbulent and challenging world of competing needs and expectations?

- **Assessments.** Assessments include national testing, formative and summative achievement, relevance, and workload.

- **Data plan.** What data do we need to collect to be able to manage our performance improvement? For whom and how does this information get collected and used? What can we stop collecting? How do we use the data to report to students, their parents, and our team?

- **Pedagogies.** How do we use engaging and proactive teaching strategies to ensure that students succeed and that staff and students remain engaged in their work?

- **Curricula.** How do we implement the prescribed curriculum and provide agency for students to deal with real-world issues? What will students need to know when they finish school, and how can we prepare them well for their life ahead?

- **Inclusivity practices.** How do we support students with special needs and their teachers? How do we resource this support and who needs to be involved in these decisions?

- **Strategic priorities.** What are our strategic priorities and how are we measuring progress as we implement our agenda? When do we decide that plans are not working and change course?

- **Support systems.** How do teachers work in teams to reduce workloads and prevent duplicating tasks? How does the team support them in times of personal challenges and adversity?

- **Professional learning plan.** How do staff access the professional learning they need? What resources are required to ensure that everyone's professional learning needs can be accommodated?

- **Leadership scaffolding plan.** How do we build leadership density across the school? How do we empower all staff to participate in decision-making processes?

- **Public relations plan.** What systems do we have in place to communicate our accomplishments to families and the local community? How do we manage stakeholder expectations? How do we manage complaints from students, families, and community members?

- **Safety plan.** Is our school safe, well monitored, and able to address personal concerns? What processes do we have in place and how prepared are we for emergencies?

- **School partnership plan.** How do we proactively engage neighborhood schools to derive mutual benefit?

Although the list above is extensive, it is neither prescriptive nor complete as these decisions or policies will be adopted on a needs basis when a lack of alignment across the school creates variation in outcomes. The plan must be owned by everyone in the school, and it should form the basis of staff meetings and professional development sessions so that the team is constantly confirming the agreed "ways we do things around here."

ALIGNING THE LEARNING COMMUNITY

Leading a learning community requires the alignment of all stakeholders to form a willing coalition that commits to balanced reform that sustainably improves student outcomes. The following reflection is from Keith Warwick, principal of Indooroopilly School in Queensland, Australia, who has documented the improvement trajectory of his school. In this summary, Keith identifies the importance of creating agency by taking a learning community approach to bring about improved student performance. Through his support, mentoring, and empowerment of staff and the inclusion of key external stakeholders, he has democratized the school improvement processes to ensure that those with the expertise and know-how are collaboratively improving practice across the school team.

A Plan for Continued Improvement

Keith Warwick, Principal

Indooroopilly State School, Queensland, Australia

Indooroopilly State School is a primary/elementary school that caters to students from Prep to Year 6. Recent years have seen rapid growth with enrolments exceeding 1,100 students. The student population is very diverse with enrolments from 54 countries and 49 language groups. The school has an excellent reputation within the educational and broader communities.

My challenge as principal of Indooroopilly State School was to generate a rationale and appetite for continued, sustainable improvement. Our strategy commenced with an exercise that asked staff to reflect upon the degree to which they felt the elements of school

(Continued)

(Continued)

improvement were aligned across each of the school's classrooms. Staff placed their individual feedback via a simple sticky dot onto a whole school improvement continuum. Staff were genuinely taken aback by the mismatch between the many measures of school success and the shared reality they had just created. I still recall the golden moment four years ago, when one of my most credible teachers said matter-of-factly to the assembled staff, "We are complacent."

The rationale for continued improvement had been generated. What followed was a carefully constructed and implemented inside-out model of change that fed the appetite for a commitment to continued school improvement. The key elements were as follows:

1. Establishment of a School Improvement Team composed of school leaders and representatives from each year level and specialist team to manage and drive professional learning in the school.

2. Development of a clear narrative by the entire staff team that captured our agreed core beliefs and commitment to move forward. This became our manifesto for action.

3. Collaborative development of a Gantt chart that outlined a clear yet responsive sequence of action in response to school improvement.

4. Establishment of strong two-way relationships with regional office and like-minded cluster schools.

5. Scheduled re-surveying of staff regarding where they saw elements of school improvement shifting.

6. Ongoing communication and revisiting with staff, students, parents, the community, the school council, and the regional office about the implementation of the work.

7. A commitment to revisiting the Gantt chart to ensure that it reflected our evolving needs.

8. A relentless commitment to staying the course; if something did not relate to our core work, we didn't do it.

Through this work, there has been a significant and measurable reduction in variability in teaching and learning practices across all classrooms. A common language regarding learning exists, as do aligned expectations of students. The presence of aligned high-impact pedagogy is observable across the school. Year-level teams have become the engine for linking a deepened understanding of the curriculum and achievement standards to the learning needs of each of our students. All teachers are members of observation and feedback triads. The Regional team partnered with the school around ways they could value-add to the school's improvement journey. Students have shifted from compliance to increased risk taking in their learning. The school's reputation garners enrolment interest from across the globe.

Keith's leadership was consistent with a more contemporary and aligned leadership model in which he focused less on leading from the front and more on building leadership density across the learning community. He epitomizes our conception of focused leadership in an era of uncertainty.

CHAPTER 3 FOCUS POINTS

1. Culture and alignment are fundamental to success in any endeavor. This is proactively and positively developed within an educational setting based on the values and practices that are prioritized and consistently challenged and revised across the organization.

2. A game plan is a comprehensive vehicle that is much more than just a priority-based strategic plan. A game plan goes much further by reforming and articulating business-as-usual classroom practices to stakeholders, in relation to how the school responds to behavior management, well-being, pedagogy, curricula, special needs, assessment, concerns, students, parents, and many other key elements of school performance.

3. High-quality teaching and focused school leadership are almost impossible without an agreed game plan that engages everyone and to which there is willing ownership, agency, adherence, and accountability.

4. Leading a learning community requires the commitment and alignment of all stakeholders to form a willing coalition that commits to balanced reform, which sustainably improves student outcomes.

CHAPTER 4

....

LEADING A RENEWED PURPOSE OF EDUCATION

Identifying Problems Is the Beginning of Learning

Yong was at a recent meeting of the advisory board of a foundation dedicated to supporting invention and invention education. The foundation has been working with higher education institutions and K–12 educators to promote invention education in schools. The participants were the staff of the foundation and advisory board members including highly successful inventors and entrepreneurs, venture capitalists, journalists on invention and entrepreneurship, and education experts. It was apparent that there was a strong dissatisfaction with education, both K–12 and higher education. A key point raised was that schools do not teach our children to identify and solve problems.

Identifying and solving problems is the most important element of invention. In a follow-up conversation with one of the advisory board members, who has more than 800 U.S. patents in the biomedical field, Yong asked how he came up with so many groundbreaking inventions in biotechnology. His answer was that he spends a lot of time observing the world of biotech looking for the problems worth solving. Then he moves on to develop the solutions.

CREATE A SCHOOL CULTURE IN WHICH STUDENTS ARE SKILLED IN FINDING PROBLEMS

Identifying and solving problems is not only important for invention but also crucial for living and thriving in our world of uncertainty (Beghetto, 2023; Zhao, 2022b). As the world continues to rethink key existential priorities post-pandemic, we must rethink our systems of education to create the problem solvers and innovators needed to deal with intractable issues such as extreme climate change and the disastrous floods, drought, record-breaking temperatures, wildfires, and melting icebergs that come with it. We need our next generations of global leaders to collaborate to address the uncertainty and deep concern in our lives. Additional political turmoil, societal divisions, changing economies, and deep-seated geopolitical conflicts contribute to heightened uncertainty. Technological changes such as ChatGPT and artificial intelligence, the global network of people and things, virtual and augmented reality, and medical technologies have already drastically changed the world and will continue to do so. The outcomes of these rapid changes are deeply concerning to most in these challenging and uncertain times.

The Arrival of Uncertainty

The world of certainty is gone. There was a time when children knew what they would do in adulthood based on the jobs their parents had. This was true for most agricultural societies and later true for societies transformed by the early industrial revolutions. Schools built to serve the industrialized societies in the 19th and part of the 20th centuries were able to teach children the knowledge and skills required for employment because it was reasonably easy to predict what jobs would exist and what skills and knowledge the jobs would require. Except for a relatively small group of people who led the world in business, innovation, entrepreneurship, politics, science, and technology, the majority of people found lifetime jobs created by others.

As a result, it should be no surprise that schools taught known answers to known problems. Schools taught the same knowledge and skills to all students, expecting them to find jobs and become good citizens. This tradition primarily continues today. Even with the emerging focus on so-called 21st-century skills promoted to support traditional academic learning, most schools don't teach students to identify or solve problems in the real world.

Living in the World of Uncertainty

Identifying and solving problems turns out to be a highly important skill for living and thriving in the world of uncertainty (McDiarmid & Zhao, 2022). Uncertainty means unknown, unpredictable, and unanticipated changes constantly occurring. COVID-19, for example, suddenly meant many people had to work from home without much warning or preparation. A small number of people were already working from home, which demonstrated that this was not necessarily problematic and, indeed, could actually be positive and advantageous for those with experience and the technological tools and understanding; however, when many more people were forced to work from home during lockdown, the situation was much more chaotic for both the workers and their businesses. They had to find new ways of working with teams, checking and reporting project progress, and finalizing projects for customers. They had to rethink their work schedule, set up workstations at home, purchase new equipment, and upgrade their internet connections. The psychological and social conditions of working from home were drastically different from those in the traditional office, which also required many workers to adapt to continue to work.

Sudden changes are happening much more frequently and affecting many more people than before. The rise of AI technology such as ChatGPT has begun to affect the lives of millions. Usual life can suddenly be altered because of flood, fire, unemployment, job changes, human conflicts, or wars. These often unplanned changes require people to quickly identify problems and develop workable solutions.

Learning to Identify Problems

In Number 8 Secondary School in Chongqing, China, a group of students chose to participate in the Innovation, Creativity, and Entrepreneurship Education (ICEE) program, designed to help students develop the ability to identify and solve problems. The program starts with seventh graders and lasts for 3 years. Identifying problems is the first step of the eight-step learning program. To begin, students are exposed to information about a phenomenon such as traffic, transportation, or anything that may be of interest to the students. For example, the first unit of learning was the fact that Chongqing, a mega-city in China, was visited much less than New York, London, and Hong Kong. Students were encouraged to come up with meaningful questions. The most obvious question for most students was "why?" but that was not a question students could immediately solve. Instead, the students continued to refine and identify significant problems they were able to solve. Throughout the process, students work to convince their partners that their problems are of significance and solvable.

The school leaders at Number 8 Secondary School created the program because they believe identifying and solving problems is necessary for innovation as daily life changes so rapidly. It turns out that solving meaningful problems in the world is what makes people authentically happy (Seligman, 2002) and perhaps provides hope and motivation. It can be both challenging and rewarding. Most of us want to make a contribution to improving the world and have a positive impact on the lives of others. This requires us to use our unique talents and passions to improve our world (Seligman, 2002).

Identifying and solving problems is an engaging learning process for all students (Zhao, 2012, 2016b, 2016c, 2016d). When students are empowered to identify meaningful problems, they are connecting their talents and passions with the real world. Many students are challenged in school and therefore disengage. They see the material as irrelevant and know that it will be forgotten after the test day. From their perspective, their time in school can seem to have little or no tangible or meaningful value. In contrast, students who are engaged in identifying and solving real-life problems have a sense

> *When students are empowered to identify meaningful problems, they are connecting their talents and passions with the real world.*

of accomplishment because their work results in meaningful solutions that have a real impact on the world and others.

Research shows that teaching students to identify and solve problems is of paramount importance today (McDiarmid & Zhao, 2022; Zhao, 2012, 2015). So how can school leaders make the necessary changes in schools so that learning takes place in the process of identifying real-life issues and problems? The change needs to start with the leader understanding that not only is teaching students to identify and solve problems important, but it does not contradict the traditional purposes of the education system. Instead, such a change helps schools to achieve their necessarily reconceptualized educational purposes.

THE PURPOSES OF EDUCATION

Every school leader understands that education serves at least two primary purposes: a private good and a public good. Schools are designed to provide each student with a set of capabilities that will serve them in their future life. Additionally, schools are designed to prepare capable citizens to positively contribute to communities and nations. To achieve these two purposes, schools adopt prescribed curricula, often determined at the national, state, or local level. Typically, education systems also use high-stakes standardized assessment mechanisms to measure how well students learn the prescribed content.

Ironically, schools in different communities and countries, with different cultures, economic conditions, political systems, and religious influences, typically promote the same basic subjects. This is why it is possible to administer international tests, such as the Program for International Student Assessment (PISA), to compare how well schools teach these standardized subjects.

Virtually all schools teach math, reading or language, science (physics, chemistry, biology, environmental or life sciences, etc.), and social studies (history, geography, civics, governance, etc.) in the hope that these subjects will prepare their students to become contributing citizens and successful individuals. To our knowledge, there is no empirical evidence that these subjects can deliver the expected outcomes of education; however, because students, parents, teachers, school leaders, and the public have been led to believe in their immutability, schools cannot modify the mandated curriculum. This does not mean there is nothing school leaders can do. What leaders do have is the power to work within the system to approach the curriculum at the macro level, instill a culture of curricular flexibility, and accept the consequences of conflicts.

SUGGESTED ACTION STEPS FOR LEADING THE NEW CURRICULA

1. Approach the Curriculum at the Macro Level

Effective and creative school leaders can lead the school in reflecting on and possibly modifying the arrangement of the mandated curriculum. This requires a new perspective where teachers within a school are provided with agency to focus on student engagement through a more personalized delivery of the curriculum. As long as schools are able to cover all the required content and skills, it should not matter how the content and skills are distributed. For instance, a K–5 elementary school should be able to look at all six grades of content and skills and empower teachers and students to teach and learn them in a manner they deem reasonable, instead of forcing them into semesters or academic years. Secondary schools need to be able to view all content as the requirement by empowering teachers and students to learn the mandated content along with their own passions in their own ways.

2. Instill a Culture of Curricular Flexibility

Once the curriculum is treated as a whole instead of being arranged for a specific semester or academic year, teachers and students have a lot more flexibility in teaching and learning. Such flexibility enables students to learn by identifying and solving problems. This starts with the students looking for real-world problems that are worth solving. Students can be given the freedom to conduct research to verify whether a problem needs a solution—or a better solution. Once the problem is identified, the students must convince teachers and their peers of its significance with evidence, demonstrating why the problem matters. The student or team of students should also provide evidence to show why they are the right person(s) to solve the problem, that is, what unique strengths or advantages they bring. Evidence should be provided to show that the problem is not only worth solving but that this is an important time to solve it. After the problem is approved and understood, the students move on to collaboratively finding a solution. From start to finish, this should be a student-driven learning experience. They will be gaining knowledge from multiple disciplines that will not easily align with curricula set up for semesters or grade levels.

When identifying problems, educators need to be considered and proactive. We should not, for instance, ask students to solve our problems. It is essential that the problems be recognized by students and solvable by students. We have seen some teachers asking students to solve problems too big, such as climate change or problems identified by organizations such as the United Nations. Indeed, problems like climate change and the UN sustainable goals are significant and worth solving, but they cannot be solved by students alone.

3. Accept the Consequences of Conflicts

Treating curriculum in its entirety will conflict with standardized testing, which is often based on grade levels. School leaders who wish to adjust the curriculum must find ways to deal with the conflicts that arise, such as potentially lower test performance because students may not have had the focus of teaching to the test to learn the grade-specific test items. That is possibly the worst-case scenario because an education that is more personalized and follows the process of identifying and solving problems will be much more attractive to students, who are much more likely to be engaged in the learning process.

Lower performance on standardized tests is more likely to happen in the early grades when students have not had sufficient time to master the necessary grammar of testing to meet high-level curriculum standards. As students move to higher grades, they will have had more time to learn the knowledge and skills measured in assessments through their problem identification and solving. The good news is that overall, problem-solving students should do much better in standardized tests because they will find meaning and purpose in their learning. Knowing that they are impacting other people's lives will make them much more actively engaged in learning. More important, this approach creates lifelong learners who can identify and solve problems independently.

SUGGESTED ACTION STEPS FOR RESOLVING POTENTIAL CONFLICTS AMONG EDUCATIONAL OUTCOMES

When making a shift from comprehensive curricula implementation to multidisciplinary problem-based curricula, school leaders should be prepared to address stakeholders' concerns about the outcomes of education. The public, parents, and possibly higher education institutions are all interested in how students are learning, and traditionally they have looked to test scores to make that determination. Relying, however, only on test scores is problematic because they only measure students' ability to perform on the tests at a given time. As a result, test scores are often an inaccurate measure of students' abilities, and they are inaccurate gauges of future potential. Moreover, test scores only measure cognitive abilities rather than other essential skills such as engagement, interests, social and emotional well-being, and the ability to identify and solve problems. Solely relying on test scores to determine student learning is just like only looking at a person's blood pressure to gauge their health: It is far from the whole picture.

Schools must pay attention to other outcomes of education, which might be in conflict. In his book *What Works May Hurt: Side Effects in Education* (Zhao, 2018d), Yong discusses four types of potential conflicts: time, short-term outcomes vs. long-term outcomes, instructional outcomes vs. educational outcomes, and cognitive skills vs. noncognitive skills.

1. Time

As students and teachers only have a certain amount of time during the school day, there is a limited number of courses or programs that can be delivered. In a classroom, when time is spent on math, that time cannot also be spent on music or art. When the time is spent on music, it cannot be spent on science. When all time is spent on academics, there is no time left for social activities. When students are spending their time on learning through identifying and solving problems, they don't have time for lectures.

Districts might require a set amount of time for certain subjects but generally allow schools the flexibility to make decisions about the time allotted to other subjects. Most education systems encourage schools to offer multidisciplinary or cross-disciplinary courses, enabling them to combine courses. Some schools have already implemented new ways of scheduling beyond the traditional 40–50 minute per class model. Block scheduling and multidisciplinary courses have increasingly become popular and more engaging. The Australian Science and Mathematics School, for example, organizes its Year 10/11 curriculum into interdisciplinary Central Studies.

In some extreme examples, schools choose to devote the majority of the school day to reading and math. As a result, these schools decreased time spent on other subjects, even decreasing the time for recess and lunch (Emler et al., 2019). In yet another example, there is a rising call for teaching coding, financial literacy, and global competence. These are wonderful courses, but adding them means taking time away from other subjects. There is also a call for adding more foreign languages and computational thinking. Again, a wonderful idea, but what subjects should be reduced or removed?

When school leaders make the decision to move to problem-based learning, they need to take the necessary steps to reorganize their teaching staff, reconfigure the daily schedule, and provide the necessary time to plan for the new curricula and the professional learning necessary to enable teachers to facilitate problem-based learning effectively.

2. Short-Term Outcomes vs. Long-Term Outcomes

Educational outcomes can be divided into short-term and long-term outcomes. The purpose of learning is to prepare for a successful and fulfilling life. It is about the preservation and transfer of knowledge and skills into the future and new contexts. It is about being able to apply one's knowledge and skills and be creative, all of which are long-term outcomes. However, to be effective, teachers must assess whether or not students are learning in the short term: each day or week, at the end of the term, or at the end of the school year.

Short-term gains and long-term gains might require different approaches. Educational psychologist Manu Kapur has conducted studies on "productive failures" in math learning (Kapur, 2014, 2016; Kapur & Bielaczyc, 2012).

He discovered that certain pedagogical approaches may produce failures in the short term, but the failures are necessary for long-term transfer and are thus productive; he called these "productive failures." Other approaches may create successful learning in the short term, but they do not translate into long-term learning. The same phenomenon has been reported by David Dean, Jr. and Deanna Kuhn in science learning (Dean & Kuhn, 2007). In an experiment, they found that although direct instruction seemed to help students learn better in the short term, learning did not transfer as well as with an inquiry-based learning approach.

> *Manu Kapur . . . . discovered that certain pedagogical approaches may produce failures in the short term, but the failures are necessary for long-term transfer and are thus productive; he called these "productive failures."*

School leaders must be aware of the conflict between short-term and long-term learning instead of only paying attention to the immediate outcomes (Kise & Watterston, 2019). It is important to introduce the topic of short- and long-term outcomes with teachers in staff meetings and personal discussions. Moving toward curricula that will achieve positive long-term outcomes is challenging, but it is a necessary component of being a successful school leader. When teachers plan for deep learning and long-term learning outcomes, students will benefit the most from their educational experiences.

3. Instructional Outcomes vs. Educational Outcomes

School leaders must be prepared to resolve the conflict between instructional outcomes and personalized educational outcomes. Instructional outcomes are the overall goals of a course of instruction, the knowledge and skills that students are expected to gain by the end of a course. Courses should also result in personalized educational outcomes, but educational outcomes are really the result of many courses, the entire educational experience, and even experiences outside school. Personalized educational outcomes are the qualities and abilities we expect children to have in life, such as creativity, entrepreneurial thinking, confidence, communicative and collaborative skills, and self-determination.

At times, instructional outcomes can conflict with educational outcomes. When we focus only on instructional outcomes, or what we plan to teach, we could be inadvertently sacrificing educational outcomes. For example, we desire creativity in our children; however, creativity can be suppressed by overteaching and one-size-fits-all teaching. In the 1970s, Penelope Peterson found through a systematic literature review that direct instruction can boost achievement test scores but can damage the development of creativity (Peterson, 1979). In the 21st century, studies by Daphna Buchsbaum and colleagues as well as Elizabeth Bonawitz and colleagues found that instruction that can teach young children immediate actions and outcomes can result in a loss of curiosity and creativity (Bonawitz et al., 2011; Buchsbaum et al., 2011).

It is easy to focus on instructional outcomes because they are assessed. It is also tempting to celebrate the achievement of instructional outcomes because they make teachers and students feel a sense of immediate accomplishment. Educational outcomes are more difficult to pay attention to because they are not usually directly assessed. We should, however, remember that there is nothing in a course that is so important that it's worth sacrificing students' creativity, confidence, self-determination, self-awareness, and engagement with schools. This is especially important when shifting teaching to supporting students in identifying and solving problems, which may result in sacrificing instructional outcomes based on curriculum standards but will result in significant gains in educational outcomes, in particular the capacity for looking for and solving real-world problems.

Paying attention to educational outcomes requires new ways of thinking about education and possibly new assessments. For example, many educational systems have identified cultivating creativity and entrepreneurial thinking as educational outcomes, but few have found an effective and reliable assessment. We have found no assessment of lifelong educational outcomes that properly lays out a pathway from one test to the next (Zhao, 2016a). There is no way to answer the simple question, "Has one become more creative or less creative?"

A possible new way to think about educational outcomes is to view them as conceptualizations of desirable qualities that may be identified but perhaps not comparatively assessed. They are perhaps a combination of many different psychological, cognitive, emotional, and social qualities that can be improved through applications in certain domains. Thus, the assessment has to be authentic through problem identification and problem solving. The assessment also has to be personalized to match the uniqueness of different students in different contexts.

4. Cognitive Skills vs. Noncognitive Skills

You have the ability to do something, but do you want to do it? Do you have the persistence to carry it through to the end? Do you have the confidence to do it? This is the difference between cognitive and noncognitive skills. Cognitive abilities are whether you can do something, and noncognitive abilities are the qualities that determine whether you want to exercise your cognitive abilities, how persistent you are in realizing your abilities, and to what extent you are confident that you can actually use your cognitive abilities to accomplish something. Noncognitive abilities have been said by some to be complementary to cognitive skills (Brunello & Schlotter, 2010; Levin, 2012).

In schools, cognitive abilities are typically measured by tests. So, in some ways, students' cognitive abilities are reflected in their test scores or grades. But cognitive skills and noncognitive qualities do not always sync together. For example, TIMSS data have consistently shown that students' test scores are negatively correlated with their confidence in the subjects and their enjoyment of the subjects (Loveless, 2006; Zhao, 2018d). PISA has shown the same trend. Students' PISA scores have been negatively correlated with life satisfaction, confidence, and value of the subjects (OECD, 2019; Zhao, 2014, 2018d). It was also found that PISA scores negatively correlate with confidence in entrepreneurial skills (Zhao, 2012).

5. Make the Right Choice

The potential conflicts between different outcomes pose a significant problem for school leaders, teachers, students, parents, and the entire education system. Everyone has to ask the question, "What matters?" Would you rather have students who are confident but do not perform well on tests, or are you interested in making sure that children are socially and emotionally healthy without pressuring them to learn for tests? The conflict between instructional and educational outcomes challenges everyone to rethink the purposes of education all the time: How important is it to have students do well on tests, and how important is it to ensure that students are happy, engaged, and confident?

These conflicts make it necessary to understand that achieving short-term instructional outcomes is not necessarily the same as realizing long-term educational goals. Being aware of conflicting educational outcomes and planning to resolve those conflicts is necessary to ensure that you are meeting all the needs of your students. As a school leader, it is your role to lead teachers and students in seeing beyond the short-term, cognitive, and instructional outcomes in order to also focus on long-term, noncognitive, and educational outcomes. There is no magic bullet for doing so. The best approach for the school leader is to bring the issue to teachers and students and invite them to consider, discuss, debate, and come up with solutions collectively.

ASSESSMENTS

School leaders need to understand that educational assessments that have been used in schools are extremely limited. Standardized tests, classroom assessments, and grades do not assess all the educational outcomes that matter. Many educational systems use standardized testing to measure literacy and numeracy almost annually. Some systems may add assessments of science and other subjects. But overall, the number of subjects assessed in standardized testing is extremely small and does not include all the subjects required at the system level.

Not only are the assessments narrow in terms of subjects, but they are also entirely focused on cognitive abilities. There is rarely a standardized assessment of noncognitive abilities or personal skills, nor are there assessments of educational qualities. If we're looking at assessment data alone, we basically know nothing about how students are succeeding in terms of long-term, noncognitive, and educational outcomes. We have been counting, but what counts has not been counted (Duckworth & Yeager, 2015; Zhao, 2016a; Zhao, Wehmeyer, et al., 2019).

Standardized tests have their purpose, but they are challenging as a reliable measure of an individual student's true abilities. Low standardized test scores should never be a catalyst to place students in isolated remediation or hold students back. Standardized test scores are, however, potentially useful as one measure of the overall learning in a school. It is useful for school leaders and teachers to look at test scores as indicators of where students are in the tested subjects and, based on the data, make decisions regarding the planning of certain learning activities. In schools where students' overall testing performance is desirable, results could validly be employed to plan for more advanced learning; however, when the overall performance is below expectation, engaging students in appropriate generative activities is much more important.

> *We have been counting, but what counts has not been counted.*

The existence, however, of a narrow set of skills and subjects of standardized tests makes us focus on these assessment results because we have a strong desire to know how our children are learning, and the only way we know how to report this is through comparative tests. As a result, schools have been required to almost exclusively attend to data from standardized tests. Educational systems and public media tend to draw the public's attention to the reputational results of standardized testing. Commercial entities such as real estate agencies also post results of standardized testing for the public. Parents are also (mis)led to look at their children's standardized test scores as the measure of success or failure. Teachers in some schools pay very close attention to standardized test scores and spend (too much) time trying to improve them.

Giving undue attention to assessment data can be unhealthy and misguided. No matter how good and important the assessment is, it does not measure the entirety of educational outcomes. When teachers and school leaders pay too much attention to improving student test scores, they can neglect other long-term educational and noncognitive outcomes that may require more time to develop and ultimately matter a lot more. Once neglected, these qualities are much more difficult to develop than knowledge and skills in a subject.

Teachers have their own qualitative assessments of learning in their courses. The lack of standardized testing in all areas of educational outcomes is not necessarily a problem: With collegial support, we can mobilize teachers to provide assessments that measure what is most important, if they do so with the understanding that the development of human qualities and skills is a long and complex process. It is, however, very challenging to apply reliable standards

> *When teachers and school leaders pay too much attention to improving student test scores, they can neglect other long-term educational and noncognitive outcomes that may require more time to develop and ultimately matter a lot more. Once neglected, these qualities are much more difficult to develop than knowledge and skills in a subject.*

to the development of noncognitive and educational outcomes. For example, how does one assess creativity and confidence continuously? There is no reliable comparative sequence and scope for creativity and confidence. The same questions can be asked of other qualities such as self-determination, entrepreneurial thinking, collaborative competence, and communicative skills.

While we wait for more research about the assessment and development of the "soft" or 21st-century skills or lifelong human qualities, teachers are in a unique position to make profile-based authentic assessments. They can engage students in problem-based or product-oriented learning (Zhao, 2012, 2016c). They can look at the products students produce against a rubric to solve authentic problems to assess students' creativity, self-determination, collaboration, resilience, and other related competencies.

SUGGESTED ACTION STEPS FOR IMPLEMENTING INNOVATIVE ASSESSMENTS

1. Personalize Assessments

Teachers who aim to instruct by teaching students to find and solve problems will have to devise contemporary approaches to assessment. Such assessments need to be deftly personalized so that they acknowledge individual students' strategies and skill development for problem solving. The traditional approach to assessment is often norm-referenced. It measures students against each other and aims to produce a rank of students in terms of their abilities. Even criterion-referenced assessments often judge students against preset criteria to see how well they have mastered the content; however, when students are engaged in identifying and solving problems, traditional assessments do not apply because each problem is different, and solutions developed by individual students are different. So, the assessment needs to fit the problem and the student. The purpose of the assessment is not to compare students or check whether they have mastered predetermined content to certain standards. Instead, it is to understand how well a problem is identified and solved, provide evidence of progress, and develop a strategy for better solutions. Thus, the assessment must be bound within the context of the problem and the learner.

2. Measure for Educational Outcomes

The assessment should measure knowledge and skills learned as well as educational outcomes such as problem finding, problem-solving skills, creativity, and entrepreneurial thinking. Innovative assessment should not simply focus on one aspect of education. Instead, it should be about all possible aspects of learning to include short-term and long-term outcomes. What is assessed should not simply be whether or to what extent the learner has mastered a skill or the knowledge; it should also include progress in a person's ability to identify and address problems.

3. Measure Noncognitive Skills

Any new assessment must measure noncognitive skills and social and emotional well-being. The assessment must include the students' confidence, interests, social and emotional well-being, as well as curiosity, creativity, and other noncognitive skills. It should measure students' intentions to identify problems and confidence in developing solutions. At the end of any stage of learning or project, assessment must include students' intentions and confidence in pursuing future learning.

4. Assess Authentically

Finally, the assessment must be authentic and based on the process and product of the learning. Thus, a personalized portfolio approach is the most optimal. To create a portfolio for academic, noncognitive, and problem-solving assessment, the students must be accountable and cogently aware of what to include, how each piece of work reflects their learning, and in what ways their learning has evolved. This approach enables students to have agency in the process of problem identification and solving, reflections on the process, and the final product or solution.

SUGGESTED ACTION STEPS FOR LEADING THE CHANGE FOR A REVITALIZED EDUCATION

1. Mobilize Teachers, Staff, and Students as Change Agents

Shifting school education toward a process of identifying and solving problems is a big move for many schools. It requires significant changes in teaching and learning, which ultimately require all teachers, staff, and students to make changes as well. The first step is that the entire school must consider and agree on the changes required. Although teachers and students will be making and implementing these changes, the school leader must take the lead to persuade teachers and students to consider the change and encourage them to explore identifying and solving problems as a new way of teaching and learning. All of this takes time, but for many schools it has been well worth the effort.

2. Empower Teachers, Staff, and Students to Own the New Course of Action

The entire school should be involved in thinking and talking about curriculum changes needed and how to realize the changes. Forums for this might include staff meetings, book clubs, research groups, small group meetings, or even a course project or entire course for students. The school leader facilitates the conversation with teachers and students, but for the endeavor to be successful, teachers and students need to buy in and own the idea themselves. They need to collectively come up with a strategy or policy for how this will be achieved. It is only when they see the benefit for themselves that it can be realized successfully.

3. Support Early Adopters

Once the game plan for change is developed, school leaders support the early adopters. In every school, there are a few teachers and students who are always on the edge, looking for new ideas and ready to make changes. These teachers and students are most likely to get started with the new approach with the support of the leader. With a few early adopters, the school runs an experimental project or "school within a school" to try it and explore and improve the project. The experiments would also demonstrate to other teachers and students how the new approach is implemented, how students and teachers feel, how curriculum and time are rearranged, as well as how assessment is conducted.

4. Scale the Innovation Across the School and Beyond

School leaders are in a unique position to spread the experimental program to the entire school and outside the school. For example, the leader highlights the accomplishment of the program in school meetings, talks about the program with system-level leaders and staff at the regional office, and creates opportunities for the students and teachers in the adaptive process to share their experiences with other teachers and students. To do so, the school leader needs to have a deep understanding and ongoing support and resourcing of the early adopters, of the changes made, of the problems raised, and of the improvements of the experiment.

5. Retain the Focus on Educational Outcomes

School leaders also interpret educational purposes defined by educational systems and pass on their interpretations to other people in their schools. High-performing education leaders have a broad and formative view of education. They are never limited by one or two narrow aspects of educational purpose, nor are they constrained by short-term test scores of students. They look at the growth of each child with a long perspective. They examine how their schools provide a healthy educational experience to support the learning and growth of each and every child.

6. Encourage Teachers to Conduct Authentic Assessments

High-performing leaders do not ignore standardized testing as one indicator of student performance and how their schools perform. They understand clearly that test scores are narrow and by no means reflect the entire story. Innovative leaders encourage their teachers to conduct additional authentic formative assessments of students. They aim to create a learning profile for each student—a profile that documents unique and valuable outcomes as well as special moments of progress.

7. Focus Teacher Evaluations on Students' Growth as Human Beings

School leaders pay special attention to teachers' relational work with students. They celebrate the human aspects of teaching, which is how teachers build relationships and provide supportive guidance to students. They are interested in teacher actions that encourage students to develop in healthy ways. In their teacher evaluation and professional development, school leaders want teachers to be proud and esteemed by helping students intellectually, socially, and innovatively grow rather than passively teaching the curriculum. They encourage teachers to pay a lot more attention to students as human beings instead of test takers.

8. Work With Community Stakeholders to Align Goals

High-performing school leaders understand that schools perform many competing functions. They want the school to do well in all aspects. School leaders lead the team to work with local communities and parents to help achieve their purposes, but at the same time, they need to maintain clear educational purposes. It is the onerous responsibility of the school leaders to ensure that the entire school and its community collaborate to make sure the different interpretations of educational purposes are truly aligned with the goal of helping students grow in all aspects.

9. Co-Create Student Learning for the Future

Finally, school leaders look to the future. They have a clear understanding of the past and present of what educational systems want, but they also understand that the world is rapidly changing. In this turbulent world, educational experiences for students need to adapt and progress as well. School leaders lead the entire staff and student bodies to co-create an education that produces competent and productive citizens and individuals for the changing world.

CHAPTER 4 FOCUS POINTS

1. Understand the contemporary purposes of education. In addition to the purposes of education reflected in the curricula and prescribed by education systems, school leaders need to plan and lead based on educational purposes that best serve the long-term needs of their students and society.

2. Rethink and reorganize curriculum delivery and engagement to make it appropriate and accessible for all students.

3. In assessment, consider the conflicting nature of various educational outcomes, some of which are not assessed in mandated standardized assessments. Focus on the long-term, educational, and lifelong outcomes beyond the immediate, short-term, instructional outcomes.

STAGE II

WHAT ARE THE MOST INFLUENTIAL ELEMENTS FOR COLLECTIVE SUCCESS?

CHAPTER 5

LEADING STUDENTS

Empower Students to Create Their Own School

At Monument Mountain Regional High School in Great Barrington, Massachusetts, a student who saw his fellow students bored and disengaged with school proposed to the school leadership that they run their own school. The leadership agreed and the students organized their own high school semester. They developed their curriculum, which consisted of individual learning projects and group projects. They hired their own teachers from the existing faculty, but the teachers were not to teach in the traditional way. Instead, they provided support when needed. The student-created school within a school was a great success and became the well-known Independent Project (Levin & Engel, 2016; Zhao, Emler et al., 2019).

Change the Curriculum

In Number 8 Secondary School in Chongqing, China, the school leadership felt that their students were too tightly controlled by the curriculum and excessively focused on studying for tests. The school principal and assistant principals wanted to give their students a new education experience, but they were also worried that big changes would hurt their students' academic performance indicated by test scores. So they started with a pilot program for some of the sixth graders. The program was named Innovation, Creativity, and Entrepreneurship Education, or ICEE. The program has three basic principles: autonomy, product orientation, and global connectedness. The most important idea underlying the program is to have students manage their own learning based on their interests and strengths.

(Continued)

(Continued)

The initial cohort had more than 120 students who voluntarily enrolled in the program. The second cohort had more students applying but was still offered to about 120 students. The students studied in the program for about 6 hours a week, while spending the rest of the time in traditional schooling. In 2022, the first cohort graduated. Despite the COVID-19 pandemic, remote learning, and limited time, the students in the program saw an awakening of agency, creativity, and improved English proficiency.

Build a School Within a School

In a private school in Perth, Western Australia, the new school principal saw the need to engage students in different forms of learning. She wanted to use entrepreneurial education to bring the changes. She brought in outside education experts, encouraged teachers and students in the school, and co-created new courses and after-school activities. She also reallocated funds to create new spaces for students engaged in entrepreneurial learning. In the end, the school's curriculum and pedagogy changed. Students are given more opportunities to discover and develop. In addition, in order to bring more drastic changes, a school within a school was built outside the primary campus. This new school, the Studio School, provides a completely student-centered education.

The above vignettes outline just a few of the numerous examples of innovations in schools across the world. Although mainstream education largely remains traditional, efforts to make changes so that students can be better served have been increasing. One of the characteristics of these changes is to create opportunities for students to become the owners of their own learning.

But not all schools are willing or able to make changes so that students can enjoy more agency and empowerment. For example, as the Independent Project became known, educators in other schools wanted to try it. In a series of articles, David Lane, a teacher in Massachusetts, recounted his multiple tries and failures to implement the Independent Project in his school (Lane, 2018). Basically, despite the enthusiasm of the students and repeated attempts by the teacher, the school was unable to make the project happen in any sustainable way. One of the reasons was the lack of support from the school and district leadership.

It is almost impossible for top-down, whole-of-system initiatives to sustainably improve outcomes in all schools through comprehensive policy and jurisdiction strategy implementation. The most effective innovation and targeted school reform happens when brave and focused school leaders empower their teachers to create evidence-based solutions to address problems of practice. Proactive change is best formulated and delivered by those who work directly with students; it is teachers in classrooms who are the real architects of meaningful change.

ONE SIZE DOES NOT FIT ALL

School leaders are typically in a challenging place when it comes to serving students well. The biggest challenge is that schools do not always meet the needs of all children because of mandated top-down, one-size-fits-all strategies that do not break with tradition nor recognize local contextual and cultural needs and challenges within the uniqueness of each school. The top-down one-size-fits-all approach has been in existence for such a long time that it has conceivably become the operating standard of school accountability. The government, education systems, the community, and the public generally accept the utility of the one-size-fits-all approach to school reform. In addition, laws and regulations have been enshrined predominantly to ensure that schools provide the same curriculum, structure their schools and students the same way, implement the same tests, and provide the same style of comparative student reports.

Students, however, are obviously very diverse in terms of their abilities, interests, and backgrounds. It is impossible for the one-size-fits-all approach to work for every school and student. Thus, virtually all schools have students who are unable or unwilling to engage, appreciate, and learn from what the school offers. As we move forward in a post-pandemic era, there has been a great awareness of the large number of students being left behind as they fail courses and tests and become disengaged from school.

All school leaders aim to support students to engage and flourish in every school, but the focus of systems on school compliance and standardized accountability measures creates significant challenges and barriers for leaders and their teams. This is not to say that compliance with laws, regulations, and system-level requirements is necessarily bad; for example, safety standards and accountability adherence are there to protect us all. However, these compliance regimes—laws, regulations, and curricula—do not collectively represent or meet the needs of all students and do not necessarily prepare all students for a drastically changing and forever uncertain world (McDiarmid & Zhao, 2022; Zhao, 2021). What school leaders need to do is to work with staff and students to develop innovative and bespoke strategic reforms to meet both needs: to fully engage all students and to adhere to the system compliance requirements.

UNDERSTAND THE LEARNERS

To engage students, leaders and empowered school staff must first understand them. Decades of research have discovered a lot about human learners, who they are, and how they learn (Bransford et al., 2000; National Academies of Sciences, Engineering, and Medicine, 2018). We know that human beings are not passive recipients of information. Instead, they actively construct their hypotheses, create their knowledge, and develop competencies. They are not solo constructors. Instead, they are social and primarily learn through social interactions. They are also purposeful and intentional learners. They construct meaning for their purposes in contexts. They want to solve problems and use their abilities to create value for others and the world (Seligman, 2002; Wehmeyer & Zhao, 2020). Simply put, students are born learners, intentional learners, and diverse learners.

Born Learners

All students are born learners because they are human beings (Beard, 2018; Ekoko & Ricci, 2014). Evolution did not plant specific knowledge and skills in human beings at birth, but it has given them instincts. One of the most powerful instincts is to learn and to create through curious inquiry, which enables human beings to survive and prosper in their environments. Without learning, adapting, and making sense of their surroundings, human beings cannot survive, let alone problem-solve and flourish.

Intentional Learners

Although students are born with a predetermined curiosity that makes sense of the world around them, they do not automatically learn everything presented to them. They are intentional and purposeful, so they only pay attention to and learn things that matter to them. Making sure that schools offer purposeful and meaningful learning to all students is the fundamental purpose of the school leader and staff. The key to engaging intentional learners is to enable opportunities for student self-determination (Wehmeyer & Zhao, 2020). Discern whether all students know why they are learning or engaged in any given activity. Ensure that all students are empowered to make meaningful and constructive decisions. Together with a sense of control over their choices and progress, students must feel that they can learn and master their desired skills and knowledge. Students also need to build relationships with others within their learning environment and feel a strong sense of belonging.

Diverse Learners

Human beings are born with diverse strengths, aptitudes, and talents. Knowing our students and what they are interested in is essential. We are also born with different dispositions and personalities. Personality refers to the characteristic patterns of thought, emotion, and behaviors of individuals. The Big Five model is the most popular personality theory (Goldberg, 1993), which describes the five traits that capture the wide range of personalities:

1. openness: inventive/curious vs. consistent/cautious,

2. conscientiousness: efficient/organized vs. easygoing/careless,

3. extraversion: outgoing/energetic vs. solitary/reserved,

4. agreeableness: friendly/compassionate vs. analytical/detached, and

5. neuroticism: sensitive/nervous vs. secure/confident.

A person's personality is considered to be a diverse combination of these five traits. A person can be high in one trait, low in another, and average in a third. For instance, a person can be very inventive, sensitive, and reserved while another person can be confident, organized, and unfriendly (Toegel & Barsoux, 2012).

Psychologists have also studied human desires—what motivates or drives people to action. Psychologist Steven Reiss suggests that there are 16 basic human desires: acceptance, curiosity, eating, family, honor, idealism, independence, order, physical activity, power, romance, saving, social contact, social status, tranquility, and vengeance (Reiss, 2000, 2004). Each individual has a different combination of these desires. As a result, our students come to school with different personal passions and desires.

Human beings have different talents, personalities, and passions. These are our sources of strengths and weaknesses. They are enhanced or suppressed by experiences (Lewontin, 2001; Ridley, 2003). Experiences are responsible for triggering the development of talents. For example, a person may be born into a family or community that does not appreciate music or is too poor to have access to music and therefore does not encounter it until later in life. If so, the person's musical talent is either never triggered or they are engaged in musical awareness, participation, and appreciation in student-centered schools. Schools have the compelling opportunity to encourage the curious minds of students to explore and experience as widely as possible to develop understandings and passions.

Experiences are essential for enhancing natural qualities, but they can also suppress the development of those qualities. People born with potential arts or sports talents are unable to discover or develop their talents in cultures, communities, or schools where they are not valued.

The majority of our youngest students arrive with abundant curiosity, active excitement, and a sense of freedom to explore. Over time, however, as mandated curriculum content and high-stakes assessment drive outcomes and pedagogical practices focusing on recall and recital, the initial curiosity, excitement, and freedom begin to diminish as students strive to meet expectations. School must be a place that provides meaningful experiences for children that may not be available at home. It should also provide collaborative opportunities for students to interact and explore with each other socially. More important, schools must be the institutions that provide equal

CHAPTER 5 • LEADING STUDENTS   79

opportunities for all children while preserving their uniqueness, which is especially important for students whose families come from challenging circumstances. In short, it must be a prime goal of schools to ensure the inherent curiosity, excitement, and exploration that young children are born with remains and is fostered throughout their compulsory time in education.

Jagged Profile

A result of the interactions between experiences and natural talents, passions, and personalities is a jagged profile (Rose, 2016) for each individual student, which means each person's abilities, interests, and personalities are not always even. A person can be very strong in math but not exceptional in the arts. Similarly, a person can be extremely passionate about languages but have no interest in dancing. In other words, nobody is average and very few are excellent at everything.

Students do not all have the same knowledge and skills. It is essential that school leaders accept that each student has their own jagged profile of abilities. Building a profile that identifies academic achievements, competencies, and interpersonal and social skills enables students to understand their strengths, passions, and challenges and to plan for the future. A student's profile is not constrained to one dimension. It includes all human dimensions—physical, cognitive, psychological, and social. Different domains interact with each other. Reporting student achievement needs to be proactive, engaging, and affirming, as opposed to a practice that does not focus on the unique achievements of the individual.

RETHINK THE VALUE OF TALENT DIVERSITY

It is very tempting for school leaders, teachers, parents, and government officials to expect that all students will engage and develop the same knowledge and skills at the same time. We expect all students to undertake the same standardized tests at the same age, and we trust that, with sufficient effort, all students will master what we teach. This education structure built upon age-based grade-level expectations for students can create anxiety and disengagement for those who need more time and personalized support to achieve in comparison to their peers. This is the standard by which we place students in gifted and talented education, special education, or divide students into different tracks, but the expectation is anti-scientific. It is impossible to expect that all students will have the same knowledge and skills as well as abilities and passions at the same age. Moreover, it is actually unproductive to have every student the same in all areas, as much as adults may wish that.

> *Human beings have entered a new world where uniqueness is more valuable than sameness. In this new world, the traditionally "unrecognized" talents and abilities have become more highly valued.*

Human beings have entered a new world where uniqueness is more valuable than sameness (Rose, 2016; Zhao, 2018c). In this new world, the traditionally "unrecognized" talents and abilities have become more highly valued. In an age of machines and artificial intelligence, every human talent that can have an impact on others is useful and admired. The talent for kicking and throwing balls was not of much value 300 years ago. It is now a multi-billion-dollar industry. The same can be said for industries built on musicians, artists, dancers, and actors. The internet and globalization have made it possible for individuals with talents to directly reach an audience beyond those who live in their local community. Therefore, a great flamenco dancer can earn a living teaching students in different corners of the world without leaving their city, and so can a person who excels at producing viral video clips on TikTok.

THE EXCLUSION OF STUDENTS IN EDUCATION REFORMS

Government-driven reforms over the past few decades have not sustainably improved education, nor have they narrowed the achievement gaps between advantaged and disadvantaged students (Bohrnstedt et al., 2015; McGaw et al., 2020; Mullis et al., 2016; OECD, 2019; Zhao, 2016a). The educational reforms and investments, no matter how great their scope, have done little to affect the quality and equity of education. A primary reason for this failure is, we contend, that systemic strategic imperatives have rarely attempted to make students the owners of their learning and partners of change (Zhao, 2011, 2012). Major reforms have played with almost all the essential elements of education. They have focused on the curriculum, tweaked high-stakes assessments, reformed teacher evaluation, held school principals accountable, and experimented with class sizes, but they have rarely involved students in designing and owning their own learning. Students have been recipients of the reforms and changes instead of architects and managers of their learning.

SUGGESTED ACTION STEPS FOR LEADING STUDENTS FOR STUDENTS

As educators and education policymakers begin to think differently about students and accept that students are natural, intentional, and diverse learners, schools will become more supportive of natural, intentional, and diverse learners. When we accept that in our rapidly changing world all talents have the potential to be valuable, we will stop insisting that student learning should be limited to a government-mandated curriculum. We should not insist on judging students by their test scores alone, continuously placing them in remediation in the hope that they will learn the mandated curriculum and receive high scores on government-mandated tests. Excellent school leaders who are prepared to educate students for their future will use their position and their talents to empower students to lead their own learning.

Below we offer several strategies for partnering with students to make real strides in improving the quality of education and learning.

Lead for Disengaged Students

Almost every school has a group of students who do not fully benefit from the enacted curriculum. Post-pandemic there is strong recognition of the high number of disengaged students who are challenged in the traditional school environment (Zhao & Watterston, 2020). The cost of living is highly challenging for a growing number, and as unseasonal climate events dominate, students are grappling with issues that pose challenges for classroom teachers. It is understandable that they are not always focused on what their teachers want them to learn. These students may also be the same ones who do not do well on standardized tests and do not behave in classrooms.

Focused school leaders in high-performing schools are challenging the traditional grade-based structure to develop unique pathways to serve disadvantaged and disengaged students. Rather than treating students as failures, they recognize their talents, interests, experiences, and external challenges, whether or not their talents match what is assessed in the curriculum. They create an integrated curriculum around a school structure that, where possible, addresses out-of-school challenges and builds on students' interests instead of providing remediation on subjects they often refuse to engage with.

Great teachers engage disengaged students and have honest conversations. They ask students about their talents, interests, and experiences and invite them to make proposals about how the school can best help them learn. School leaders in these schools could also empower teachers to introduce the students to some new possibilities, such as building a safe and personalized school within the school or allowing the students to have more flexibility in choosing their courses. There are many other possibilities, but the key is to deliberately empower the disengaged students to solve their real problems with the support of teachers, which will build resilience, hope, and inclusion and lead to better connection and opportunity.

Instill a School Culture in Which Students Lead Learning

School leaders work with teachers to empower students to become owners of their learning. School leaders need to develop a school culture that recognizes the importance of students as owners and managers of their learning. In this culture, teachers and staff are supporters, guides, coaches, and resource curators for students, but learning is primarily the business of students. Each student is supported to develop and manage a personalized learning or personalized education experience plan under the guidance of teachers. This learning plan is strengths based and passion driven. At the beginning of each semester, students should work with their teachers or advisors to decide the courses they will take and other curricular and extracurricular activities they plan to engage in, with a focus on exploring and developing their strengths and passions. Students then take on the responsibility of reviewing their progress and revising their plans, if necessary, with their advisors (Zhao, 2016b, 2018c).

Rethink Teachers' Responsibilities

Personalized learning requires school leaders and teachers to rethink the distribution of teacher responsibilities and workloads so that they can assume the role of advisors or coaches. Each teacher will be assigned a group of students to work with in the capacity of advisor or coach. This assignment is not instructional but relational. As advisors and coaches, the teacher's job is not to tell students what they should do. The advisor's job is to talk with students to explore what students want and need to do. This arrangement enhances the teacher-student relationship and increases student engagement because students are now part of their learning process and have an adult in school who genuinely cares about them and gets to know them as empowered individuals.

Empower Students to Partner in Governance and Decision Making

Student-centered schools go much further than adapting and adopting innovative programs and personalized learning. Contemporary schools are beginning to focus on the inclusion of students in all forms of traditional decision making and school governance. We have seen student representatives on school boards and committees and on school councils, but very few schools embrace student participation in all school matters. An example of a democratic school that embraces this model is Summerhill School, a private boarding school in Suffolk, England, where all students and staff meet each week to discuss and decide issues that members of the school raise, such as bicycle parking. The decision is made via votes and each student has one vote, as do teachers.

Student agency and empowerment can be much more than becoming the architects of their own learning through inclusion in decisions traditionally managed by leaders, staff, and community members. Examples of proactive and authentic student leadership we have seen in schools include the following:

- being included on selection panels for new teachers and professional staff,

- planning and design of new classrooms and buildings,

- selection and purchasing of technology and school resources,

- advising on and dealing with student behavior misdemeanors,

- planning major events,

- leading and coordinating school assemblies,

- reviewing school data and performance,
- creating an advisory group to support teaching and learning across the school,
- school policy and implementation, and
- student-led proposals for courses, clubs, and other learning programs.

Collectively empowering and including students across the school in decision making provides a level of engagement, innovation, and inclusion that builds community and a culture of teamwork and authenticity. Schools are created for students, so it is important that students' voices and their ideas, feedback, and choices are included in decision making.

Although not all students can be included in advisory groups, it is important to democratize school decisions by using class time to review school practices, decisions, and opportunities. It is fundamental that every student understands and participates in these democratic processes.

It is also important for students to exercise their agency in terms of their preferred learning styles, curriculum content, and passions. Encouraging students to understand *how* they learn in addition to *what* they learn is important in a student-centered democratic school. For example, a student could ask to take an online course that is of great interest to them and meets the curriculum standards, instead of the equivalent course offered by the school. A group of students may propose replacing one course with another course they develop. Another group of students may propose a project using the school library or garden as resources. The school leader, teachers, and students together should develop assessment criteria to ensure they are meaningful and productive learning experiences.

Student participation in school operations creates a shared agency in all aspects of the school, including decisions regarding curriculum and extracurricular activities. Students might offer their own courses to others. Invite students to weigh in on important matters such as the school library, campus, facilities, classrooms, and computer equipment. Students could be organized into committees to make improvement plans, in collaboration with school leadership and teachers.

Involving students in decisions concerning schools not only enhances their sense of engagement, it also brings new ideas and resources to the improvement of schools. When students are engaged in decision making, they develop a sense of responsibility and the realization that their decisions affect others. If rules are made with students or by students and they are placed in the role of implementing the rules, teachers will benefit from student buy-in and cooperation. Students and teachers should review rules collaboratively and remove rules that do not make sense. For example, rather than banning smartphones, students and teachers could come up with a plan for how they could be used constructively for learning and in a way that will not cause disruptions. This requires students to agree to use phones responsibly for digital literacy and only according to the rules agreed upon by the class (Reddy et al., 2020; Zhao, 2020).

Work Collaboratively to Create Innovative Programs: The Why, When, Where, and What of Contemporary Learning

Due to the dangers of COVID-19, the great majority of schools used technology to provide remote learning in which students worked from home in the care of guardians or on their own. While this was highly challenging to many teachers and students, it has become clear post-pandemic that reverting to all pre-COVID practices is not practical for most schools and students.

Prior to COVID-19, innovative schools were already connecting with student collaborators internationally using online curricula along with an abundance of curated websites and learning resources not always available in traditional school courses. We quickly learned through necessity that many students took the opportunity to learn anytime, anywhere. They realized that they could focus on learning what they are most interested in, and they have reconsidered *why* they learn, which is much more than simply preparing for future employment.

Many student-centered schools are focusing on the why, where, when, and what. There should be no going back to the conservative pre-COVID-19 classrooms where teachers lead from the front, teaching the same concepts to learners who may or may not understand or engage. It's time for schools to take a leap and lead the rethinking of schooling rather than maintaining the status quo with minimal change. It is time to create innovative programs with teachers and students without being constrained by the perception that all students, parents, or teachers are opposed to creating significant change.

To meet the needs of savvy and connected students, take the opportunity to enable trailblazers to create a school within a school that is different from the traditional school. Let those in the school within a school operate independently so that it does not directly impact those who are happy with and engaged in the traditional school.

Recruit students and teachers for the school within a school who seek new educational approaches and new learning experiences. It should be open to anyone who wishes to join, but they must understand and be willing to diversify their learning experiences within the what, when, where, and why framework. Ensure that the activities of the school within a school are made visible to the entire school so that other teachers and students are aware of the innovations, which may result in welcome changes to the existing school. Build support by letting the whole school community understand and appreciate the innovations so that they, too, might be inspired to request those changes for themselves. A school within a school makes innovation an invitation rather

> *A school within a school makes innovation an invitation rather than an imposition on teachers, students, and parents and thus prevents possible resistance. It is a co-construction with staff and the school community rather than an isolated top-down intervention.*

than an imposition on teachers, students, and parents and thus prevents possible resistance. It is a co-construction with staff and the school community rather than an isolated top-down intervention. The entire school should be aware of the agreement to construct the school within a school.

Another strategy is to work with teachers to examine their curriculum to determine whether they need all their allotted time to teach mandated subjects. If the teacher finds that there is extra time available, the school leader can ask the teacher to consider reducing their teaching time by 20% and setting aside that 20% for student-led learning. Fridays could become student-led learning days, when students are empowered to pursue their own learning plans, offer their own courses to each other, or engage in personally meaningful learning activities.

Engage Students in Curriculum Planning

A school curriculum must prepare students to become good citizens and successful lifelong learners. All students must engage in essential learning to function well as citizens, but what makes them successful is individual and personal. Thus, schools should require students to take the same subjects, but not all the subjects should be the same for all students. Imagine a curriculum that has two parts. Part I is the national and state or local requirements for all students; Part II is the personalized curriculum desired by individual students. Engagement really matters, and providing opportunities for deep learning in subjects and courses that interest students is an essential element for success.

Use Students to Teach and Mentor

Asking students to teach courses, manage libraries, keep classrooms orderly, take care of networks and computers, and so on may sound inappropriate or a misuse of child labor, but these duties are beneficial to engage students who have decision-making agency in activities that have real outcomes and gives students a sense of responsibility. The opportunity to serve others teaches that their actions can have a meaningful impact and that it is up to them to deliver meaningful and quality work. These activities give students a sense of participation in the school, and by extension their community. When students are given the responsibility to participate in the running of the school, they know they are contributing to and bettering their own community. The outcomes of their actions give students a sense of accomplishment. When they are able to see the results of their work, they know that the quality and the diligence they put into it makes a difference. These activities give students a sense of ownership and the knowledge that they can do meaningful work that leaves an impact on the world. Finally, these activities give students a sense of relevance to others and the school community. Their actions are connected to the real lives of others. These understandings are necessary for students to further develop their capacity for self-determination and enhance their engagement with schooling.

> *We have observed students offering consulting services to other schools; we have also seen students organizing conferences, teaching courses, managing school schedules, serving as librarians and lab assistants, and cleaning classrooms.*

We have observed students offering consulting services to other schools; we have also seen students organizing conferences, teaching courses, managing school schedules, serving as librarians and lab assistants, and cleaning classrooms. Students are a very powerful group of the teaching force that school leaders should consider.

Enable Peer Tutoring

Reduce the burden on teachers in schools by having students tutor each other. Peer tutoring, as a form of education, is very powerful. Richard Elmore (2016), a former Harvard professor of education, observed peer tutoring in Mexico. In rural villages, children tutor each other in all sorts of subjects. The program is called *Tutoria* and was found to have a tremendous impact on the rural children who took part, especially girls. The tutoring not only helps the tutee but also the tutor. Elmore, a professor who had observed thousands of classes, wrote that *Tutoria* or peer tutoring is much more powerful and meaningful than many traditional classes.

Peer tutoring has not always been formally used as part of school education. Some teachers use advanced students in their classes as teaching assistants to offer help to students who need it. We have also seen schools that enable advanced students to offer tutoring during lunch hours; however, rarely have we seen schools that systematically institutionalized peer tutoring.

There are different ways to organize peer tutoring. Invite students to show that they have knowledge and ability in certain topics. Publish the topics on school websites, social media, and other announcement venues so that interested students can sign up to be tutored. All students are encouraged to both tutor others and be tutees. Schools could, for instance, create a peer tutoring cohort. With the leadership of a few teachers, peer tutoring would include only willing students, without affecting others.

The reason for introducing peer tutoring is to utilize and reinforce the students' abilities and interests to help themselves and each other. It is not only to introduce a new form of learning but also to reduce the time teachers are responsible for remediation and teaching.

CHAPTER 5 • LEADING STUDENTS

CHAPTER 5 FOCUS POINTS

1. High Expectations: All students are natural and intentional learners, but it is important to note that learners have innate differences, which means they are not equally good in every domain, nor are they equally engaged.

2. Student Profiles: Discard the goal of making every student equally good in the same knowledge and skills. Work to help students develop jagged profiles of capabilities.

3. Inclusive and Diverse: Lead students to personalize their learning. Encourage *all* students to take control of their learning and create the space for them to do so, ensuring that diverse students are supported and included.

4. Provide agency and empowerment to all students to democratize the school's decision making and governance through meaningful engagement and opportunity.

CHAPTER 6

LEADING TEACHERS AND OTHER PLAYERS IN SCHOOL

Support Innovative Teachers

Don Wettrick is one of the best-known teachers in enabling students to follow their passion and develop entrepreneurial spirit and skills. He started as a middle and high school teacher in Indiana and is now a well-known consultant, speaker, and author. He is the founder and president of StartEdUP, a global network of innovators, educators, and some of the best-known entrepreneurs. He has led classes of students to pursue entrepreneurship education. According to Forbes columnist Robyn Shulman (2018), Wettrick is "one of the few teachers I've ever met who brings education, hands-on entrepreneurship, real-world change, innovation, and collaborative skills into his classroom."

Although many teachers might have ideas similar to Don Wettrick's, not all teachers have had the opportunity to implement their ideas. Wettrick was fortunate to have focused school principals who supported and encouraged him. His students embraced his new style of teaching and actively took advantage of the opportunities he created. In the book An Education Crisis Is a Terrible Thing to Waste: How Radical Changes Can Spark Student Excitement and Success, *Yong and co-authors documented a number of teachers who deviated from traditional curriculum and pedagogy and brought significant innovations to their teaching (Zhao, Emler, et al., 2019). These teachers were empowered and fully supported by their school leadership.*

TEACHERS ARE THE MOST IMPORTANT ASSETS IN SCHOOL

Teachers deliver learning. They directly convey the mission and vision of the school to students through their teaching. Their interpretations of the curriculum, their view of learning, their perspectives on students, and their opinions on education are all evident in their teaching. How teachers teach and interact with students defines the learning environment and culture of the school and, therefore, they are the most important members of the team in the school. School leaders are judged according to the quality of outcomes and the sincere care for students that teachers put into their work. The success of any business or organization is directly related to its customer service, which fundamentally applies to all schools.

Leading teachers is not an easy job because teachers are unique human beings with different skills, knowledge, attitudes, values, passions, and interests. It is fair to assume that most, if not all, teachers want to have agency and purpose. As we saw during the COVID-19 pandemic, teachers *en masse* demonstrated that they are innovative, resilient, and caring—they responded to school disruptions promptly, adopted remote learning, and showed extra care to students and parents, without much preparation.

Leading teachers should not be didactic. It does not involve giving out mandates. Sometimes, as in the case of Don Wettrick, innovative teachers just need license, resources, and support. The command-and-control approach does not sustain practice because teaching is not a simplistic job that can be prescribed. Teachers express themselves through their individual personalities, talents, compassion, and interests. They need to be empowered, recognized, respected, and valued even when they may be struggling. Targeting or highlighting poor teaching does not directly lead to excellence. Excellence is derived from ongoing communication, support, mentoring, and understanding. Just as good teachers demonstrate care and promote well-being for their students, so it is that school leaders need to demonstrate their compassion and coaching capacity to lead a culture of teacher performance improvement. Leaders must believe that all teachers are able to improve and therefore provide support and mentoring for them to grow and realize ongoing development.

Post-pandemic, teachers in general are tired, frustrated, and constrained (OECD, 2020). They have been subject to numerous government-led innovations and changes, mandatory requirements, and test-based accountability measures in addition to societal changes, school disruptions, and everyday student issues. They have also been the target of criticism regarding educational outcomes, the promotion of new skills for students, and school reforms. In addition, they have been the audience of many professional development efforts aimed at changing their practice and adopting new pedagogical tricks and curricular adjustments.

Leading teachers, thus, cannot be through more mandates, more top-down accountability measures, and more external professional developments. Successful school principals treat teachers as self-determined individuals who want to create value for others and who do the best for their students.

LEAD TEACHERS AS SELF-DETERMINED INDIVIDUALS

Thinking of teachers as trusted, empowered, and self-determined team members is foundational to successful school leadership. Treating teachers as a compliant and homogenous group waiting to take instruction from the school leader suppresses innovation and the capacity to exercise their professional judgment. Teachers, like most people, have the desire for self-determination. They innately have a desire to do things that have value to themselves, their colleagues, and their students. They require real agency through which they can make decisions to achieve their students' goals and realize their potential. They need volition in decision making. Forced actions do not have the heart or passion of the actor.

Teachers Have Agency

Assess the degree of agency teachers have and how they use it. It can be a challenge for leaders to seek constructive change from their team if they are prescribing teachers' practice and invoking the use of strict and stringent accountability measures that are seen as compliance. A similar undesirable approach uses test scores as the indication of teaching effectiveness and mandatory professional development programs.

School leaders need to resist such institutionalized and ineffective approaches. Providing supported opportunities for innovation is infinitely more productive than invading teachers' space by mandating what they need to do in their classes or how they must manage their students. This, however, does not mean that as a proactive and empowering school leader you cannot assist in building teacher capacity or encourage them to change teaching practices to improve performance.

Make it a practice to regularly talk with teachers to recognize their work, communicate your concerns and encouragement, provide support, and show your appreciation. Start with the belief that no one wants to do a bad job. Respectfully offer the support teachers need to improve while empowering them to exercise their agency.

Giving teachers agency to make teaching decisions builds trust and collaboration, but it is the leader's fundamental role to make sure that all teachers are working faithfully in keeping with the school's game plan. When working as a team, the value of the work lies with realizing better outcomes through the endorsed school game plan built around the vision for the school. Only when the entire school is doing well, and all members feel valued for who they are, can individual teachers feel good about themselves.

Teachers Want to Do Better

The psychological theory of self-determination (Ryan & Deci, 2017) suggests that teachers are self-motivated to build mastery and improve. To do so, it is essential that they understand why they are doing what they do. How do you engage teachers in improvement, especially those who have been ignored, criticized, or even punished for low performance? Address concerns about teacher performance carefully and respectfully, with trust as well as support instead of criticism or condemnation. It is never a promising idea to simply demand improvement or threaten with punishment.

Externally delivered professional development sessions can be inspiring, but they are not likely to result in long-term growth in teachers. Great schools should make sure to create opportunities for teacher learning and growth, but not simply through one-day or one-time presentations by so-called experts. Every teacher should have a plan for professional development designed and implemented with other teachers in the school and based on each teacher's unique needs in dealing with challenging circumstances in their classroom.

Teachers Want Relationships

Self-determination theory also suggests that humans want relationships. We all have a strong desire to seek belonging and connection. Teachers want to have solid work relationships. They want their work to be relevant to others and want their purposeful actions to be meaningful and recognized. They require and deserve agency, mastery, and relationships to achieve self-actualization and self-transcendence by improving their practice. It is the school leader's job to instill confidence and opportunity for teachers to be able to refine their unique skills so they can address the common goal of improving education for all students no matter the starting point.

SUGGESTED ACTION STEPS FOR BUILDING A PROACTIVE TEAM CULTURE

The school principal's most important task is to lead by example to build a healthy and proactive culture across the school and community where all teachers can contribute within a functional and mature team environment.

Build Relationships With Each Teacher

Build relationships with every teacher by getting to know them and understanding their passions and needs. Then instill a democratic process in which all voices are recognized and appreciated. You can do this in team-building meetings or retreats where all participants are encouraged to value a team approach that recognizes the talents and aspirations of their colleagues. These meetings, in time, need to become safe havens for teachers to understand and share their challenges and seek help from others.

Build Time for Teacher/Teacher Interactions

Building time and space for teacher interactions is a powerful way to facilitate and maintain proactive relationships. A common meeting place within the school is required for teachers to interact professionally and feel confident to share their teaching problems of practice. As Linda Darling-Hammond has repeatedly stated throughout her influential career; "Teaching is a team sport."

Give Teachers Opportunities to Fail

Building a culture of support and teamwork is challenging work and it takes time. We all have a fear of failure at times, but connected teams provide support and commitment to each other, which replaces a sense of failure with the opportunity to rethink and reform. Teachers need the courage to admit to a colleague that they do not know what to do next to support a challenging student. They will only do so if they are confident that their vulnerability will be supported. It only takes one negative experience to revert to privatizing their practice. As great teachers do with their students, teachers need to be given as many chances as they need to try new strategies and ask for help. This is the hallmark of high-performing schools. It is the principal's role to maintain safety and positivity throughout the school community. It starts with building confidence, and then providing multiple oppor-

> *Teachers need to be given as many chances as they need to try new strategies and ask for help . . . It is the principal's role to maintain safety and positivity throughout the school community. It starts with building confidence, and then providing multiple opportunities for sharing, trust, and collaboration.*

tunities for sharing, trust, and collaboration. This kind of collaborative culture thrives on honest and supportive feedback. In this way, the principal becomes the conductor of the orchestra in which everyone stays in harmony and in tune.

Build Collaboration Into the Structure and Organization

Rethink the organization of your schools. Find ways to organize your school to make building communities and relationships easier. Traditional schools tend to put teachers in their isolated classrooms, thus making teaching a privatized, invisible, and individual act. High-performing schools, however, encourage teachers to work in teams to bring about a desired change. For example, many schools have cross-grades or subject teaching arrangements whereby teachers have time to work together to design and develop teaching approaches. The teaching-research teams in East Asian schools, where teachers of the same subjects or grade have weekly meetings to discuss and plan their teaching together, are great examples of this practice (Lewis et al., 2013; Paine & Ma, 1993).

Create Opportunities for Teachers to Build Relationships Around Common Professional Interests

Activities such as research groups or teaching built on common interests can be powerful ways to help teachers develop relationships. Teachers can form groups to investigate common problems of practice by connecting with universities and embracing relevant research. Providing time to build collective capability as an investment in the school culture will result in better outcomes for students. Funding sabbaticals or time releases for teachers to meet with experts to find solutions to local practice problems is a high-value investment in classroom teachers and their students that is becoming more common in high-performing schools.

Build in Time for Teachers to Cultivate Professional Relationships With Peers Outside of School

Teachers are professionals who need to participate in professional activities and build relationships with other teachers outside the school by meeting online and attending relevant teaching and learning conferences. Provide resources for teachers to participate in local, national, and international professional communities. Through these relationships, teachers can keep up to date with new research, new pedagogies, and innovations in teaching and learning. Through online professional activities and conferences, teachers are able to share innovations in the school with the outside world, seek feedback for improvement, and spread the message of innovation. The external communities are also psychologically valuable as they provide a sense of belonging to a larger network of teachers all working toward the same goal: empowering students as architects of their own learning for lifelong success. As a school leader, it is your job to prioritize, fund, and encourage such opportunities for teachers.

Adjust Teaching Schedules to Build in Time for Sustainable Improvement

Build a learning community where teachers engage in a process of long-term and sustainable improvement. Provide access to contemporary evidence-based resources for teachers to explore problems of practice. Teachers should be given time to explore and to construct solutions, which may mean adjusting teaching schedules and timetables. Ideas for school reforms should ideally come from the teachers, not the school leadership.

This can be a challenge for some leaders, who desire to be at the forefront of strategy and new initiatives. Educational improvement is a team activity that requires working without letting ego take over.

SUGGESTED ACTION STEPS FOR BUILDING AND REALIZING A VISION WITH TEACHERS

Educational changes start with a vision: a common understanding of where we want to go and a pathway to get there. A vision is the conceptualization and imagination of a future (Fullan, 2014). The school leader's role is to prompt the team with ideas and opportunities to consider specific plans for change, but the creation of collaborative plans cannot be realized until, and unless, the leader co-constructs the strategy with teachers. Only when teachers (and others in the school) have agency and rally behind the vision is there a foundation upon which it can be realized. It must be collaboratively developed and owned by the entire school community.

Engage Teachers

Building a vision starts with knowing and engaging teachers and other players inside and outside the school. This includes providing teachers with the opportunity to research and explore as they identify the problems of practice to be addressed. They must be empowered to come up with their own solutions or even the identification of new problems. A key to the success of these deliberations is that the teachers feel inspired and supported to make a difference. The school leader facilitates suggestions and recommendations but never imposes them. Our definition of great leadership is ensuring teachers and others believe the change plan originated from them and was their idea all along.

Strategic Change Is an Iterative Process

Building a strategic vision is an iterative process. Start with a holistic review of relevant data and shared observations of possibilities for change. Then explore educational research and practices. Discuss and debate the different educational proposals as they are applied to the school context and the identified problems.

There can be many different perspectives, and thus different views of the same data and observations among teachers and other school staff. For example, some teachers may be more interested in the engagement and long-term growth of students, while others are only interested in academic performance and thus pay exclusive attention to test scores. Teachers may be interested in behavior compliance without considering that rule-breaking students may be seeking outlets for their creativity. Thus, discussions about data are contentious. It is necessary for teachers holding different perspectives to participate respectfully in debates so as to understand each other's perspectives and learn new ways of looking at the data. This may not immediately lead to consensus, but eventually, consensus must be reached to build a shared vision or to enact a new or revised aspect of the school's overarching game plan. As school leader, encourage teachers and staff to openly express and debate their views. Encourage teachers and staff to do more than simply challenge each other. Implore staff to examine different philosophies of education, different perspectives of teaching and learning, different views of subjects and curriculum, and different ideas about schools from experts and researchers so the debates are informed discussions that lead to sound decisions.

Stay Deeply Connected to Your School Context

These debates and discussions should not be theoretical. They need to be based on the context of the school. Every school is different: the socioeconomic status of students, academic performance, parental involvement, and teacher engagement all affect the status of the school and school culture. When discussions and debates are deeply connected to the school, new perspectives will emerge, and new solutions will develop that apply to your specific context.

Rethink Pedagogy

Pedagogical approaches are central to student engagement, motivation, and achievement (Hattie, 2023). The artistry of teaching is, unfortunately, not always at the forefront of educational discussions where student performance is considered. Pedagogy is somewhat of a catch-all term, but it is much more than teaching techniques, styles, or performances. Each teacher's pedagogic approach is fundamentally an extension of their unique personality, interpersonal skills, relationships, theories of learning, and personal commitment. Pedagogy also includes assessment, feedback, consolidation, and other practices adopted by teachers to maximize learning. At a simplistic level, pedagogical practice can be thought of as a continuum, with teacher-focused direct or didactic instruction at one end and student-led discovery learning at the other. The former emphasizes well-organized content, teacher-delivered lectures, and compliant students, while the latter is student centered and inquiry based. There has been much debate about the effectiveness of the two polarized approaches (Zhao, 2018d). The reality is that pedagogic approaches and the many other identified practices can be effective, but ideology and devotion to exclusive approaches limit the agency of both students and teachers.

Direct instruction takes less time and can teach more students. Its effectiveness is largely in passing information to students. If the assessment is about information memorization, direct instruction is more effective. Pedagogical decision making is complex and best left in the hands of those in the classroom where collective decisions are made to impact the performance and achievements of unique students who learn at different speeds, in different ways, and with different challenges. School leaders need not use their position to mandate approaches; engagement and ongoing conversations with teachers are fundamental as the school game plan is developed to ensure that experience, research, and positive practice inform school-endorsed pedagogical approaches. In this way, teachers need to be given the opportunity and information so that they can have productive and collegial conversations, which help develop a common vision of teaching in the school (Hattie, 2023).

This iterative process is also a process of empowerment through which the school leader engages teachers and other players to ensure that they are the collective change makers and they have the space and agency to make changes. When the school has developed a shared vision, the entire school should have an empowering climate for improving education. The vision must be adventurous but practical and needs to be deeply connected to student learning. Essentially, the vision, which is not static, is owned and evolved by all players in the school and benefits everyone.

Empower Teachers to Innovate

Teachers often do not feel empowered to innovate or be creative in their teaching, nor do they always seek authority or power to make changes. As a result, their innovations are often passively constrained to their own classes. To enable teachers' innovative capacity to be unleashed, school leaders must make it clear that all teachers have agency and support to collectively engage in reform through research, practice, and by collecting ongoing classroom-based evidence.

> *This iterative process is also a process of empowerment through which the school leader engages teachers and other players to ensure that they are the collective change makers and they have the space and agency to make changes.*

Innovation without trust, time, and agency is difficult. New teachers learn from seasoned performers to adapt to "how we do things around here," which might stifle their potential for innovation. Build a culture of innovation so that teachers straight out of graduate school and credential programs are not prevented from sharing their evidence-based new ideas. Provide resources and systems so that mature and seasoned teachers can mentor and support new teachers in finding their way, understanding the game plan, and developing an understanding of what works for individual students in your school setting. Treat them not as apprentices but as innovative talent to be cultivated as valued members of your student-centered culture. The opportunity to develop new and innovative ways of doing things is what is needed as teachers in many countries are departing from the profession due to overwhelming workloads and a lack of professional recognition. Leaders must believe that teachers are capable of collaboratively innovating from the bottom up—with their support.

Acknowledge and Protect Innovations

Support and encourage teacher innovations by showing appreciation for those who innovate. Acknowledge their work in public, within the school, and in the larger community to stimulate the interest of other teachers. Promote schoolwide events to display the innovations of teachers to inspire the entire school community. Create a culture of innovation by actively building a formative accountability system with teachers that rewards and supports innovation and improved student outcomes. Proactively work to remove innovation constraints. For example, when teachers come up with innovative ideas but need changes in scheduling, curriculum implementation, or ways to organize students, actively enable them to do so by focusing on changes that are beneficial to students. Protect innovative teachers from external interference. When innovation happens, some parents or students may be challenged because they do not necessarily agree with or understand the innovation or change of practice. This may elicit complaints or posts on social media about the changes or specific teachers. Local media might get involved via the agitation of vested interests. This is when teachers most need your support.

School leaders who promote innovation and constructive change must deal proactively as gatekeepers with those who may be inclined to want their children's school to be more like the school they went to decades ago. Always refer to reforms, changes, and innovation as the school's program of work rather than isolating teachers leading the project.

Proactively inform the community regarding emerging innovations. Facilitate the creation and sharing of an evidence-based iterative assessment to improve innovative practices and student engagement. Experienced and astute school leaders learn to anticipate potential complaints and opposition and work to explain the changes to related stakeholders to preempt concerns. Innovation or reformed practices often challenge perceived curriculum arrangements imposed by the education system, which can cause discomfort in system leaders and bureaucrats as well as parents. Find ways to work within the system to enable teachers to innovate and thereby benefit students.

Tips on Proactively Managing Innovations

- Proactively inform the community about emerging innovations well ahead of their implementation. Explain the reasoning behind the change and the evidence that supports how the innovation will better help the school meet its goals.

- Anticipate possible external concerns and preempt challenges by regularly sharing the strategic imperatives, progress, and evidence.

- Ensure that innovations operate within the parameters set out by the system.

- Proactively engage stakeholders at the district level before implementing new strategies.

Remove Pressures From High-Stakes Testing

Removing the pressure from high-stakes testing is another one of the many ways to create space for teachers. Standardized testing has become a tremendous imposition on teachers. School leaders can exacerbate the pressure by holding teachers directly accountable for test results. Although we believe that relevant data is essential for evidenced-based innovation and student progress, we believe that personal accountability for high-stakes national and international testing is of questionable value in truly improving education, as this can constrain teachers' freedom to explore more productive and meaningful change.

Many focused and high-performing school leaders emphatically articulate that focusing exclusively on improving standardized test scores by narrowing the curriculum and "teaching to the test" is not the purpose of the school and thus is not included in teacher evaluation. All leaders primarily believe that student learning is the most important task of the school, but standardized testing does not always accurately and comprehensively reflect that. Nor, in most cases, do standardized tests take into account the impact of socioeconomic status on overall outcomes. High-performing leaders engage their teachers to work on diverse ways to assess students. We all know that what gets measured gets done, so developing a local assessment that has validity and accuracy is a meaningful task for teachers. The Faculty of Education at Melbourne University has initiated the New Metrics project to work with schools across Australia to design new assessment profiles for their students. About 40 schools have joined the project for more than 3 years. Their purpose is to develop new assessments that measure performance capabilities beyond the traditional pass/fail measurement of skills. Through the engagement of teachers, schools can minimize assessment pressure so that they have more agency to provide targeted evidence of student performance across the spectrum of learning and development.

Remove Traditional Boundaries

Traditional teaching tends to limit teachers' agency in their classroom to prescribed subjects or courses. In contrast, with collective agency and an innovative game plan, the curriculum could be reorganized and adapted to reflect the needs and passions of students. Given license, teachers in innovative schools combine multiple disciplines into new and more tailored courses. These new approaches enable teachers to work together to use their uniqueness to contribute to self-managed student learning. For example, we have seen a school in South Australia, the Australian Science and Math School, that has changed its curriculum by merging multiple subjects into projects so that teachers work in project teams. Teachers from different subjects work together to guide and support students in their development of products. Relaxing the delivery of the curriculum enables teachers to have more space to create innovative practices.

In Summary

Teachers require liberation, respect, recognition, inspiration, and, most important, realistic remuneration. To attract high performers to the profession, school leaders need to give their staff agency and license to improve practice to better engage students and prepare them for the opportunities they will experience throughout their lives.

Once the traditional boundaries that cause teachers to believe their role is limited are removed, they have more space to exercise their agency and identified expertise to work on bigger projects that involve multiple disciplines. Most important, school

> *Teachers require liberation, respect, recognition, inspiration, and, most important, realistic remuneration. To attract high performers to the profession, school leaders need to give their staff agency and license to improve practice.*

leaders need to build trust among teachers. Teachers need to believe that the school not only wants to innovate to make a difference but also that boundaries will be removed, where practical, with time and resources allocated for research and exploration.

SUGGESTED ACTION STEPS FOR LEADING TEACHERS IN THE NEW CONTEXT OF EDUCATION

Classroom teachers have traditionally been thought of as the source of knowledge in front of students and as the authority over students and their classrooms. Education programs and credentialing courses have focused on ensuring that teachers master their subject matters to be able to teach. They learn about learning, teaching methods, and classroom management, as well as assessments and evaluation; however, the context of education has changed.

A recent major change impacting everyone is the availability of knowledge online and the arrival of ChatGPT and similar language models (Zhao, 2016d, 2021). There is no question that human knowledge has been increasing at a dramatic pace, but more important is the easy access to this knowledge, which continues to grow exponentially. Today, anyone with internet access can access most human knowledge, with artificial intelligence such as ChatGPT making knowledge so much more attainable than traditional search engines. Most students in developed countries have easy access to accessible knowledge online.

Another change is the format that knowledge takes. Human knowledge can exist as books, papers, artwork, human memory, PowerPoint presentations, online encyclopedias, videos, audio files, games, and so on. Students can access both primary sources and prepackaged forms of knowledge such as video lessons presented by experts, online courses, textbooks, and other resources. Students who are motivated to learn about any given subject can find a source to learn from. With ChatGPT and other AI tools, students can find answers to practically any question they have.

The third big change is the availability of experts, teachers, and tutors online. Technology has made it possible for people to communicate globally, which means that anyone with expertise can teach or tutor anyone anywhere. Various companies have organized online teaching and tutoring across national borders to bring expertise to students in most countries.

These changes in accessibility, format, and availability of experts make it possible for school leaders to lead teachers to innovate to better serve all students. The fact that the classroom teacher is no longer the only source of knowledge makes it possible for students to exercise their self-determination to seek additional learning opportunities from a vast range of sources on their own.

The pervasive sources of online knowledge and expertise provide school leaders with the opportunity to work with teachers to shift from their traditional position of providing instruction to more democratic positions such as personal coaches, resource curators, global connectors, project managers, and community builders.

Appoint Teachers as Personal Learning Coaches

Personalization of learning may be one of the most important roles for today's teachers. In the new context of education, students are fast becoming the owners of their learning. Education is strengths based and passion driven, and learning is problem based and oriented toward creating solutions for unknown problems. Thus, the first enabler all students need in this context is a teacher who understands them as individuals. The teacher guides them in developing their strengths and passions, points them to resources, directs them to meaningful and productive activities, and supports them in creating value for others and the world.

Through personalization of learning, teachers work with individual students and their parents or guardians to develop a profile of each student. The profile should include interests, passions, strengths, and activities to further develop interests and strengths. High-performing teachers work to identify resources and pathways for each student and help them identify their strengths and passions. Teachers also mentor, encourage, and challenge students to reach their goals and to translate their strengths and passions into something of value that will make a difference.

Appoint Teachers as Resource Curators and Global Connectors

The role of resource curator enables teachers to bring learning resources to students to support and personalize their learning. There are countless resources online and in the local community for students, but the help of teachers is important to sort out what resources are valuable and relevant. Teachers work with students to identify, evaluate, and curate resources.

In this age of globalization, learning can be internationalized: Learners can expand their learning community to include global peers and collaborators, which means they create value through their learning for people with different perspectives and experiences. Students can learn from global resources and participate in global projects, working with experts and peers from around the world. This requires teachers to become global connectors.

Commission Teachers as Community Builders

Students utilizing external resources are free to learn from anywhere. Teachers as community builders can help students engage in learning that takes place within a community, to ensure it is meaningful and creates teams built on diversity and differing expertise. The teacher is the leader of a community of learning in which students with different approaches to learning can access knowledge from different resources, but they come together and work with each other to decide the learning outcomes. The community also provides a place for students to present their findings, conduct evaluation of their learning, and receive feedback from peers and the teacher. Students may learn individually or in small groups within the community, but they are all part of the community designed and led by the teacher.

For teachers to adopt and exercise these new roles, schools have to change. School leaders in this context empower teachers and students to undertake the changes themselves. This includes meaningful changes in curriculum delivery to make spaces and opportunities to create collaborative and meaningful student-led projects that are engaging and make a difference. For example, schools can reorganize curriculum into broader stages by learning in subject teaching blocks that focus on continuity and sustained learning. Schools can also prioritize personalization to allow students to lead their own learning and enable teachers to become personal consultants. The book *An Education Crisis Is a Terrible Thing to Waste: How Radical Changes Can Spark Student Excitement and Success* (Zhao, Emler, et al., 2019) gives examples of teachers and schools that have embarked on the journey to make radical changes in the new context of education.

Constructing a vision with teachers and collaborative innovation is the beginning of strong and empowering leadership. Enacting the vision and making iterative changes is the continuation of leadership. The effective school leader is always in the process of working with teachers and other school community members to co-construct, enact, and test the commitment to the vision.

CHAPTER 6 FOCUS POINTS

1. Teachers are the architects of education in schools. Thus, school leaders must work to ensure that all teachers are motivated, supported, and engaged in improving education in the school.

2. Effective school leaders believe that all teachers are willing and able to improve if opportunities are provided. They give teachers meaningful feedback and individualized professional development to ensure their success.

STAGE III

HOW TO AVOID THE PITFALLS THAT PREVENT SUCCESS

CHAPTER 7

·····························

LEADING THROUGH FORMATIVE ACCOUNTABILITY

Shifting the Locus of Control

Fear of Failure

When Jim was the director-general of Australia's Queensland Department of Education, he used to spend time visiting schools. During one of his visits to an inner-city primary school, he was being guided around by a team of school leaders, members of the student board, and community members (despite his request for a low-key visit designed to ensure minimal disruption). As he was being deftly guided to an external door of a new library, he caught a glimpse across the other side of the room of a special needs child pulling over a shelf of books. In the blink of an eye and without anyone acknowledging what could have been a very serious incident, the door was shut, and the principal moved like an elite ballroom dancer to usher him in a different direction, hoping that he had not seen the incident. He's sure it was a source of great disappointment to the principal when he asked to see if the boy was OK (which, thankfully, he was). The principal was clearly worried that he and the school would be judged harshly and rated accordingly due to this unfortunate occurrence. Fear of failure is a massive impediment to school improvement, and this culture must be turned around before we can develop the education systems that we are seeking to create.

"What gets measured gets done and what gets rewarded gets repeated" (John E. Jones, III) is a truism that—perhaps unfortunately—shapes education practice and performance across many countries. It is, therefore, imperative that what we measure in schools is what matters for all students to optimize their life chances and opportunities. The work of schools and educators can be driven by external high-stakes measures that do not always capture the full experience, capability, and needs of all students. Student performance is, of course, impacted by a diverse range of issues, including innate student characteristics, family and school socioeconomic background, and other factors such as disability, attendance, and inclusion. Schools that are high performing (often due to high socioeconomic status) are more often rewarded and attract a greater percentage of higher-performing students, which creates an abundance of challenges for schools in more challenging areas.

In short, how we measure school performance and the outcomes we prioritize have a significant impact, for better or worse, intended or not, on teachers and students in all schools. Measuring the things that matter influences equity provision and highlights the current inequities across schooling sectors. School leaders and teachers need to agree about what matters for students and the school community so that what matters is prioritized, formatively measured, and understood. Resultant evidenced-informed teaching and local reform then bring rewards as student performance and engagement improve. In this way, measurement is not imposed, bureaucratic, or a burden for busy teachers. Measurement becomes the research that turns into new knowledge and teacher know-how. Empowered teachers then drive strategy by collaborating with each other to better support student growth and engagement.

Educational systems, parents, students, communities, and other stakeholders all expect schools to excel at delivering outstanding educational results to every student. Some of the expectations may be reasonable and some may not. School leaders are held accountable for ensuring that the school meets these systemic and community expectations.

It is virtually impossible for a school to avoid being externally accountable—nor should they want or need to avoid being accountable. The educational system and bureaucracy, as well as parents, community leaders, and the media, have clear expectations that schools must meet. External school accountability is often dominated by standardized testing, systemic compliance, and high-level policy implementation. Although standardized testing provides benchmarks for comparing school performance, the school leader must communicate that there are additional, often more robust, measures of school performance and student success. Effective school leaders can seize control of accountability and showcase performance and engagement measures that credibly identify student progress, achievement, and connectedness. Effective school leaders are those who effectively communicate the value of internal measures and outcomes to all stakeholders. They prioritize and negotiate the best accountability measures for their schools to ensure that students are defined by much more than their summative high-stakes test results. Effective schools demonstrate confidence to all stakeholders and earn their support by upholding meaningful measures that recognize the whole child from a sensory, social, emotional, and academic perspective. They focus on formative measures that identify abilities, skills, passions, and personalized achievements rather than relying on summative testing that highlights deficits. Great schools build an assessment culture of innovation, learning by curiosity, measuring what matters, and then doing whatever it takes to respond effectively.

The notion of external accountability across education systems and within schools is often the cause of great stress and fear as leaders and teachers feel unfairly judged. Traditional accountability mechanisms often result in summative judgments and point-in-time assessments of isolated practice and performance. These review processes vary from system to system, but they are usually conducted by officers external to the school. Many teachers and principals worry that the reviews do not always add much personal value, they create a lot of work both in the preparatory and review phases, and recommendations are often heavily influenced by the previous experiences and views of the reviewer(s) rather than focused on an unbiased and objective review of the evidence, practices, progress over time, and stakeholder feedback.

SUGGESTED ACTION STEPS FOR LEADING FOR MORE EFFECTIVE ASSESSMENT

School leaders are responsible for ensuring that each student in their school progresses over time to reach an optimal standard. Ydesen and Bomholt (2020) support this view when they note,

> Schools should be accountable to their communities for the goals which they serve . . . . accountability for the sake of educational goals should be seen not in terms of tight control mechanisms and fixed structures, but rather in terms of the establishment of a dialogue between schools and their various communities . . . . The key elements in effective school-based accountability are firstly that the community has access to information on educational goals, processes and outcomes, and secondly that there be clearly defined and recognised means by which the community can respond to that information. (p. 55)

This includes working with the school community to review school practices, policies, resource deployment, and the culture and motivation of staff to ensure the best possible outcomes. We all want to know that we are doing the best we can and that our collective effort is having a positive impact, so it is important to have comprehensive systems in place that provide up-to-date feedback and data that can drive renewed action and confirm progress.

Work With the Community to Identify Outcomes

When beginning a new leadership position, one of the first actions school leaders need to take is to generate authentic community consultation and decision making to determine which essential outcomes should be the focus of their work. Which capabilities, competencies, and dispositions will stand students in good stead in later life, and which externally driven outcomes will potentially distract the school from its mission? The school leader then needs to share the consensual agreement with the entire school, staff, students, parents, school board, and the community it serves. Providing agency to stakeholders breeds engagement, motivation, and proactive accountability. The school leader also needs to lead stakeholders to build their capacity and skills to attain the determined outcomes.

Motivate Staff to Take on an Evaluative Mindset

Identify and utilize internal and external accountability processes to motivate staff to take on an evaluative mindset to measure their own success and innovation. In contrast to top-down accountability processes that identify where the school is failing, formative accountability is focused on cyclic and contextualized evaluation and investigation of the school (not the teacher) to measure the impact of strategic initiatives, which can then be proactively modified based on relevant evidence. In many schools, external, summative accountability creates pressure and stress for staff, but it need not be punitive. Instead, it should be affirming and the basis for direction setting and reform. Formative accountability empowers, whereas exclusive, isolated, top-down accountability often creates fear, inertia, and poor morale.

Working Hard Is Not High Performance

The problem with being the accountable officer is that as leaders, we often assume we know how well the organization is doing based on observation, intuition, or gut feeling. Many leaders fall into the trap of equating teacher effort with performance. Just because people are committed and work hard does not mean that their impact is being optimized. Hard-working leaders immersed in the day-to-day whirlwind need to lead teaching staff to put in place objective systems and processes to obtain regular, independent, and valid feedback that will confirm and optimize performance levels.

Move From Deficit Accountability to Proactive Accountability

Traditionally, accountability processes have been high-stakes, one-off events where jobs were potentially at risk. These processes were carried out by the "system" to ensure compliance and policy adherence, define practice, and verify whether school performance met the expected standard. School leaders often fear that promotional opportunities will evaporate if their school is not rated highly, and we have sat on enough promotion panels to know that data-driven results often do matter when it comes to selection. To succeed under this dynamic, school leaders tailor school strategy to meet the expectations of these inspections.

To build a proactive and collaborative culture, deficit accountability practices from a critical analysis perspective model need to be constructively shifted to a proactive, empowering, and solution-focused approach. Internal school accountability mechanisms need to be introduced with ongoing cycles that confirm performance standards and provide external validation along with teacher-driven opportunities to refine practice for further improvement.

Accountability outcomes in education look different across the various contexts in which schools operate, but parents, the media, and other key stakeholders will still be looking for comparative progress on an upward trajectory. Schools need to have a range of information systems in place to measure performance from social, well-being, emotional, and academic perspectives. It is fundamental to lead the development of contemporary accountability processes that focus not on an external system but instead on empowering local school staff to ensure that they become the architects of their own school improvement strategic trajectory. To reorient the school accountability culture, take ownership of the process and demand that reviewers and system leaders become key contributors to ongoing improvement processes designed at the local level. Ensure that schools and school systems build an authentic culture that changes the accountability narrative from an external quest for perfection to an internal thirst for quality feedback and support upon which to shape future improvement and direction.

MEANINGFUL FEEDBACK

Abraham Maslow encapsulated the elements of the human condition with his Hierarchy of Needs. Maslow believed that a person's self-esteem was positively influenced by a sense of belonging, which was achieved by feedback and recognition. We all want and need to know how we are performing and whether we are making a difference. Quite simply, Maslow contended that we need to feel valued for the contribution we make. From a teacher and school leader's perspective, ongoing formative feedback and proactive accountability reviews can serve this basic human desire. The feedback required, however, must be focused on enhancing impact and building esteem and capability, or else the process can be incredibly underwhelming and dissatisfying, as the following (real) example reveals.

> *Lead the development of contemporary accountability processes that focus not on an external system but instead on empowering local school staff to ensure that they become the architects of their own school improvement strategic trajectory.*

Jim once visited a very large, isolated rural school very soon after moving into his new job as the director general of the system. After a few hours of looking at classrooms and facilities, he was taken into the principal's office and was immediately surprised to see the room full of colored balloons and streamers all over the place. He was initially impressed to learn that the decorations (probably strategically) were left over from the previous night's party for staff to celebrate their latest school external,

(Continued)

(Continued)

top-down accountability review, which had yielded a report with green ratings for each of the eight review domains. This was a much-improved set of ratings from the previous review a few years earlier, when "red traffic lights" dominated the report. Naturally, everyone was thrilled about this "surprise" outcome and that they had "passed" the external review, even though previous challenges remained. He, of course, added his congratulations, which he assumed contributed to the morale that was already palpably high!

Once he arrived back in his office a day later, he wanted to know more about this audit process. It turns out that the audit process was mostly focused on school inputs: policies, practices, curriculum provision, pedagogical and assessment frameworks, strategies for stakeholder engagement, and so on. The review was very light on evidence of student and teacher progress and impact. It did not seem to confirm that the array of green-rated inputs was making a difference.

He was therefore amazed to be shown that the system performance data relating to the school in question revealed a completely different story and would certainly not have attracted any green ratings whatsoever. He was confronted by a comprehensive and well-intentioned review process that had been developed with great fanfare and political acclaim but, at least on this occasion, it had comprehensively provided a "false positive." The review had overlooked the fact that literacy and numeracy data had not improved at all since the previous review 3 years earlier. What clearly had happened since the previous review was that the principal and staff had faithfully implemented all the structural recommendations provided by the previous review team. It was obviously valuable for morale and school marketing, but it provided minimal evidence and feedback upon which a program of student performance improvement could be founded. The review was built on the assumption that the provision of all the inputs in the review framework would be the recipe for school success.

If only it was that easy! The misguided focus of the subjective and input-driven review process was the fault of the system; it was a wasted opportunity and provided minimal return on investment to ensure that real student progress built on feedback-based reform could be implemented.

"The contexts in which a treatment is implemented can mediate its effect and cause adverse side effects. In one context, the treatment may result in its intended main effect, while causing harm in another context" (Zhao, 2018d). There is no one-size-fits-all improvement formula that reviews inputs and effort as proxies for success.

SUGGESTED ACTION STEPS FOR ADDING VALUE AND MINIMIZING FEAR

Most school systems are too big and unwieldy to effectively exercise top-down control to improve the performance of every school and ensure that every child is receiving a quality education. Such systemic approaches lead to fear, distrust, and compliance. School leaders soon learn from their colleagues what reviewers are looking for, and through adherence to the frameworks that guide the process, the whole exercise can degenerate to passive participation to get through the process. That is, schools organize their one- or two-day examination or review to be a special event where everybody has been rigorously prepared to give the examiners the best possible view of the organization, instead of showcasing the day-to-day problems of practice and warts-and-all events that characterize the challenges and unpredictable nature of all schools.

Pasi Sahlberg (2010) describes *intelligent accountability* as balancing qualitative and quantitative measures to build mutual accountability, professional responsibility, and trust.

> Intelligent accountability utilizes a wide variety of data that genuinely expresses the strengths and weaknesses of a particular school in meeting its goals. It combines internal accountability—consisting of school processes, self-evaluations, critical reflection, and school-community interaction—with levels of external accountability that build on monitoring sample-based student assessment. (p. 53)

He describes an accountability model that is proactive and balanced between the mutual obligations of the bureaucracy and the school.

> Intelligent accountability also stresses the principle of mutual responsibility. This means that accountability dynamics can be regarded as a two-way process. On the one hand, schools should be held accountable to decision-makers and the community for the overall outcomes of schooling. These outcomes, collectively defined by the school and their community stakeholders, go far beyond the student-achievement results that remain the focus of external standardized tests. Expected outcomes include non-cognitive areas, such as social skills, moral values, and aspects of personality not assessed by current tests. On the other hand, decision-makers, authorities, and school boards should also be held accountable for providing schools and their students, teachers, and principals with the resources, conditions and opportunities needed to attain jointly agreed educational goals. (p. 54)

It is time to ensure that unhelpful school accountability reviews no longer act as a handbrake on school improvement. Recognize the power in using internal processes to liberate leaders and their staff to lead their school's transformation, instead of being driven only by top-down benchmarks and standards that do not always reflect the unique challenges and evidence-informed practices of teachers. It is the key work of the school leader to work with staff to turn school reviews into catalysts for change, opportunities, and improvement rather than constraints on progress.

Break Away From Command and Control

School leaders need to break with the command-and-control and the teaching-to-the-test traditions. Experienced principals usually learn too late in their career that they, not the bureaucracy, have the power to effect real change in the school. Through deft leadership, accountability processes can become key opportunities for growth and renewal when all school staff become co-creators focused on measuring the things that matter to drive their school's upward trajectory. System direction needs to empower those closest to the classroom to make the key decisions that will deliver better outcomes.

Involve External Reviewers

When schools review their own practices and performance, it is essential that teams contain external people who can bring different perspectives to the process. There is a place for external peer reviewers and leaders from within the system who can ensure internal school review teams operate consistently and objectively, and stay focused on the school's strategic priorities. External critical peer reviewers included in all internal school review teams should provide balance and a fresh perspective, and bring confidence and reliability to the accountability processes. They also ensure that processes and staff do not become self-serving, unconsciously biased, or beleaguered by school and system constraints. Most important, however, all seconded peer review supporters need to undergo a school orientation to ensure that they can effectively add value to the review process and assist the school team.

Review Annually

It is important for an individual school that reviewing progress is not just a cyclic investigation that occurs every 2 or 3 years. By creating a comprehensive and scholarly annual reporting process, schools with a deep analysis of all available data that matter can be a collaborative venture in which everyone involved learns, shares, and responds. In this way, schools can leverage best practices to improve performance and outcomes for all.

> *By creating a comprehensive and scholarly annual reporting process, schools with a deep analysis of all available data that matter can be a collaborative venture in which everyone involved learns, shares, and responds.*

Include Both Formative and Summative Data

To obtain regular and valid feedback on school performance, it is essential that schools provide teachers with relevant formative and summative data to measure student progress and teacher impact. Most schools do have these valuable instruments in place, but it is important to conduct regular internal evaluations and share them across the school community. In this way, community confidence will be sustained, and school staff will use the evidence to drive enhanced teaching and learning. Using newsletters and meetings to share outcomes with stakeholders creates trust and understanding, which brings with it credibility and an enhanced reputation.

Focusing on the Strategies for Accountability and Improvement

Other strategies that can assist with local school performance improvement and accountability include the following:

- Solicit external reviews. Invite neighborhood school leaders and/or teaching staff to review selected aspects of school practice on a quarterly basis.

- Solicit visitor feedback. Develop a simple feedback questionnaire for all visitors to the school, to gather data on things they noticed and perceptions they developed during their visit.

- Conduct internal and external observations. Visit other schools to examine their relevant practice and context. Collaboration with others across systems and sectors is important for professional learning and benchmarking local performance.

- Use data to update the community. Ensure that at every school council or board meeting performance measures and relevant school data are presented and discussed so that the school community is aware of and involved in improvement processes.

Find and Negotiate the Best Accountability Measures

If a school focuses less on high-stakes test results, the leader must shift the community's emphasis on high-stakes assessments as a measure of internal accountability. Make a convincing argument for student-centered measures of accountability. Stakeholders such as the school community and local media can use these measures to tout the accomplishments of the school and promote real estate values.

Creativity, entrepreneurial spirit, critical thinking, collaboration, and other similar competencies can be important outcomes for which schools should be held accountable. These are important 21st-century skills and are increasingly recognized as being teachable and highly valuable in the new world where technology has replaced or will replace human beings in many industries.

Include Students in Assessment Decisions

Engage students with assessment and data collection. In an evidence-based environment, give students agency to understand performance and decide what should be measured and why it matters. Students should become assessment literate so that they can understand what progress they are making and then be involved in classroom and parent-teacher discussions about designing pathways to improvement. Too often we do things *for* students instead of doing things *with* students. Engagement and ownership are the first steps to independence and personal accountability. Before we move to improve test scores, we should consider putting students at the center of internal review processes.

It is not so difficult to find additional student profile measures for which schools should be accountable, but it does take time for school leaders to develop consensus with stakeholders. It is also important for school leaders to discuss potential new accountability measures with students.

Additional ideas for measuring data that leads to a culture of success include the following:

- Student engagement, attitudes, confidence, participation, diversity, and inclusion

- Parent and community participation and engagement

- Student and teacher culture and well-being

- Student behavior management and associated conditions

- Student leadership participation

- Community service and out-of-school learning (e.g., languages, sporting pursuits, arts)

- Complaints and management resolution

SHARED ACCOUNTABILITY PROVIDES DIRECTION THROUGH AGENCY

Accountability should and must be shared. No one person bears all of the responsibility for the elements for which the school is held accountable. Although the school leader does not carry all of the responsibility, they are the driver in charge of developing a culture of shared accountability.

Shared accountability is much more than each person taking part in the process to answer to accountability measurers. It is about stakeholders understanding their roles and responsibilities within the school. When individuals know their responsibilities, they then understand how to hold themselves accountable for producing the agreed-upon outcomes. The school's improvement plan should clarify the common vision and lay out the responsibilities of each role to avoid confusion and slippage.

Student growth and learning is the most important outcome of schools, so any accountability plan should ensure that students understand their roles and responsibilities as learners. The school should work with each student to develop their learning pathways. We want students to help shape their progress and how they will be assessed.

The school leader's role is to provide agency to everyone involved. Agency engages people as it gives them a role in design, decision making, and assessing performance. Teachers and students then are empowered to work together to develop a culture of agency in which they have the time and space to exercise self-determination, pursue purpose, and develop mastery and relationship.

FORMATIVE AND SUMMATIVE ACCOUNTABILITY

Formative accountability is primarily about providing feedback (Australian Institute for Teaching and School Leadership [AITSL], 2014). It is a periodic process of gathering evidence and reflecting on the data in regard to the intended outcomes. Formative accountability leads to reviewing and reforming the game plan, how it is enacted, and how evidence is analyzed. The purpose is not to judge individuals; rather, it is to make necessary changes to ensure the implementation is on the right track and also help the individuals to become better at what they do.

Formative accountability is a dynamic process. School leaders should use formative accountability to have conversations with teachers, to learn about their own personal growth or difficulties, and to help them examine their innovations, practices, and plans. It should be treated as a very significant process of teacher support and professional development. Teachers, when they are engaged in frequent proactive and evidence-informed conversations about their performance, appreciate the feedback and aspire to do better. It is important that school leaders do not treat formative accountability as a tool for controlling or manipulating teachers.

Students should go through formative accountability as well. It is important for students to be constantly aware of their learning and progress. Based on the results of the assessment, students, teachers, and parents can all revise their plans and learning outcomes.

The school leader is central to the creation of an evaluative culture across the school. The leader must have a strong sense of the community aspirations for students and the progress of the school. Regularly engaging with stakeholders across the school community is fundamental to measuring the things that matter and drawing in the findings to enhance practice and outcomes.

> *The school leader is central to the creation of an evaluative culture across the school. Regularly engaging with stakeholders across the school community is fundamental to measuring the things that matter and drawing in the findings to enhance practice and outcomes.*

KNOW-HOW AND HOPE INSTEAD OF FEAR AND RISK AVERSION

Accountability is not only about holding schools responsible or maintaining the status quo. It is about encouraging schools to make changes, to grow, and to better serve and educate the community. The changes we want schools to make should be future focused and based on hope, aspiration, and problem-solving know-how instead of fear and risk aversion.

Changes should be driven by hope for a better future, but too often school changes are driven by fear of being left behind or of failure to deliver certain outcomes. Hope and preparation for success are powerful drivers for change. When people have agency and are motivated to be part of the solution, the drive is strong, innate, and persistent. Success is a continuous process.

Change should be driven by the accumulated know-how of a team that uses their assessments and evidence base to drive professional development for teachers as they collaboratively identify what works. A higher level of expectation is built upon collaboration, teamwork, and collective efficacy to ensure the best education for all students. The changes schools are held accountable for should come from within the school instead of being imposed upon the school.

Focus on Accountability Best Practices

1. Regular internal school reviews are welcome opportunities to check the school's engine and see if it needs a tune-up!

2. Well-targeted and unbiased feedback is the spice of life. We all grow if we have an honest assessment of how we are performing and a knowledge of what needs to be done to further improve.

3. The locus of control for cyclic review processes must be internally retained by the school. Constructive reviews are designed to empower school staff to become architects of their school's improvement. It is not a time for top-down external direction or control.

4. A school review is conducted *for* the school, not *to* the school. Schools should be constantly internally reviewing and evaluating their performance, impact, and processes. If the system works as it should, then an external review should confirm that your school is on the right track.

5. Experienced and unbiased reviewers will assist with a school review, but it is the empowered school staff who must take ownership of what needs to be done. It is essential that the evidence- and data-gathering processes form the basis for school-driven innovation, remediation, and solution development.

6. Accountability and school review processes are formative, moment-in-time judgments based on the collection of objective evidence that is robustly tested. They should not be isolated, independent assessments based on assumptions or opinions.

7. When accountability processes reveal the need for intervention, then it is incumbent on the school leader to provide additional resources and support to enable the school staff to bring about the required improvement.

8. School review and accountability processes should not be merged with individual performance management processes. Review processes that judge people are not helpful. They create fear, subversion, and nondisclosure.

9. Review processes are to judge the overall quality of student performance. Every member of the school staff is collectively a part owner of that performance.

10. There are rarely summative assessment regimes that can adequately capture a school's performance level. Rankings, traffic light gradings, numerical scores, critical descriptors, or any other comparative analysis will immediately devalue and undermine a review process. Every school is unique, and it therefore requires continuous review, which leads directly to contextualized findings and considered recommendations that are designed to lead to action.

In short, we need to change the narrative of school accountability from assessment and "gotcha" moments to professionally enabling schools to get on with their business based on relevant, reliable, and challenging feedback.

CHAPTER 7 FOCUS POINTS

1. Change the narrative of accountability from mandated high-stakes standardized tests to a culture of formative accountability aimed at improving education instead of evaluating individual teachers and students.

2. Focus on reviews that provide constructive and meaningful feedback, giving teachers the information they need to make changes for improvement.

3. Work with all school stakeholders to find and negotiate what to measure, how to measure, and how to use the data. Measure that which is important and that which has been previously neglected.

CHAPTER 8

···································

LEADING FOR SUSTAINABILITY

Embracing Disruption and Crisis

The AI-Powered School

In June 2023, Gabriel Rshaid e-mailed Yong the manuscript of a book titled The AI-Powered School: A Hands-On Guide to Integrating ChatGPT and Artificial Intelligence in Schools. *Gabriel is the head of the Global School, a new school in Argentina he co-founded after being the headmaster of St. Andrew's Scots School in Buenos Aires, which is one of the oldest bilingual schools in the world. Gabriel has been a progressive leader of schools and has written multiple books on technology and education. In this new book, Gabriel offers practical guidance and sample lesson plans for teachers to use ChatGPT in their teaching. The guidance and lesson plans cover the core subjects of reading, writing, and math as well as other subjects such as history, social and emotional learning, physical education, and the teaching of ChatGPT. Gabriel also discusses more challenging issues such as academic integrity, cheating, and how to move toward teaching metacognitive skills.*

Gabriel is an innovative school leader who thinks about "futureproofing" his school. ChatGPT was only released to the public in November 2022. It took him less than 7 months to write a book about how schools and teachers should think about ChatGPT and AI and to offer educators suggestions for using AI in education. We do not expect all school leaders to move so fast, but we believe all school leaders should always be thinking about the future and what to do to ensure that their teachers and students are embracing the future instead of being stuck in the past.

> *The evidence in evidence-based education, evidence-based leadership, and evidence-based practices is all based on the past. Evidence can only be gathered when something has already happened. As a result, education leaders must seek inspiration from the past to make plans for the future.*

As the future is unknown and uncertain, school practices are based on what we do know: the past. The evidence in evidence-based education, evidence-based leadership, and evidence-based practices is all based on the past. Evidence can only be gathered when something has already happened. As a result, education leaders must seek inspiration from the past to make plans for the future.

To draw from the past requires school leaders to have a future-oriented mindset and capabilities to understand what events may or may not matter for the future of students and the future of schools. Gabriel's work on ChatGPT is a great example. He clearly believes that this AI technology has significant relevance to schools and is likely to drastically change the future for teachers and students. He may be off the mark, but given what we know about the rapid escalation of learning technology and its impact on the world, he is right to be questioning the impact it is having on education and the potential for increasing significance in the short and long term.

What are the key challenges in this disruptive era of smart machines, an existential climate crisis, rapid and ongoing changes to employment, social media's promotion of fake news, and destabilized international relations that will significantly affect the future of today's students and the operations of schools?

In this concluding chapter, we revisit our thinking in previous chapters and provide our future-focused view of the most significant changes needed in education. As we noted earlier, we need to foster a generation of problem solvers, innovators, and leaders to unite the world as we seek to provide positive futures for all. Our best hope for united responses to the intractable and escalating problems we face is for schools to prepare our students to move education from the certainty of the past to solutions for the future. It is a time for the elevation of school leaders to focus on what we know and to guide their community to determine a desired future.

We begin with some of the major changes of the past few decades and how they have affected school leaders' thinking about curriculum, pedagogy, assessment, and other aspects of school operations.

IMPACTFUL CHANGES

Over the last few decades, the world has gone through significant changes that affect how we live, work, and play. These changes include COVID-19, ChatGPT, re-globalization, climate change, and failures of education reforms.

The COVID-19 Pandemic

The COVID-19 pandemic created a remote-work class (Lund et al., 2020). In our recent past, a small percentage of the workforce carried out work at home. Then the pandemic forced millions more people to work from home. This trend might continue as businesses discover the benefits of remote work and workers get used to and get better at remote working. Some of these remote workers, after more than a year of staying home with their children, have found out that they would rather have their children spend a few days a week at home learning remotely under their supervision.

The COVID-19 pandemic resulted in a universal experience with online learning. Although remote learning during the pandemic may have been among students and teachers from the same school, the reality is that learning can be global—with students, teachers, and learning resources located in different parts of the world.

The COVID-19 pandemic taught people about uncertainty in an unprecedented way. Although we have talked about our world being uncertain, few of us had experienced such drastic and quick changes prior to the pandemic. Schools across the globe were closed overnight for a few weeks in some places and for more than a year in others. Virtually all educators, students, and parents faced the reality that schools could close anytime. The sense of uncertainty in which we now live should make us better prepared for future disruptions.

We are seeing constructive changes to the delivery of education as schools harness the opportunity that was forced upon them through the pandemic to think about the possibilities of learning anything anywhere, any time, and with technology that provides us access to virtually anyone across the world. There are increasing examples of districts moving to fewer in-school days per week, with a capacity to work from home, as schools are facing staff shortages (Watterston & Zhao, 2023).

ChatGPT and Artificial Intelligence

ChatGPT and AI, based on the evidence so far, seem to hold tremendous power to transform human society and schools. Within a month of its release in November 2022, more than a million users signed on to ChatGPT. They used AI tools, for example, to write poetry, essays, and computer codes; pass high-stakes exams; complete Google computer coder interviews; and complete homework and assignments or write recommendation letters. Every day AI usage in schools and by students increases.

ChatGPT is only one of numerous AI programs. AI is behind Siri and Alexa. It supports Google Translate. AI manages delivery workers. AI reads medical images and texts. It monitors the movement of people. In China, it tracked the locations of people during the pandemic. No one knows exactly how and where AI will be used and what the impact on human life will be, but it is certain that the impact, like the impact of previous technological revolutions, will be big.

Schools must proactively deal with ChatGPT and other AI technologies because of the immediate and future significant impact on students, teachers, teaching and learning, as well as the operations of schools. During the pandemic, virtually all schools used technology to support online learning while school buildings were closed. However, the use of technology in schools has not resulted in significant and fundamental changes in education. When the pandemic forced schools to close, technology was used in unprecedented ways, but unfortunately, those changes were largely de-emphasized by many schools when they returned to the old normal of in-person learning (Ginsberg & Zhao, 2023; Zhao et al., 2015).

It is not certain that ChatGPT and AI will drastically change schools in the short term. Some school leaders immediately banned it; some school leaders are not sure what to do about it and therefore have done nothing. Other school leaders, eager to determine the potential of ChatGPT and other emerging platforms, asked teachers and students to think about strategies for applying it to improve learning outcomes. The impact will depend upon access to technology, school policies, and the actions of school leaders, teachers, students, and parents, but we can all agree that AI is here to stay and will rapidly continue to develop. There is also no question that ChatGPT and other emerging AI software will disrupt human jobs. That, in itself, will be a significant challenge for schools, and it requires urgent attention to ensure graduating students are not just prepared but they have the evolving skills, knowledge, and adaptive capacity required to enter new jobs and professions.

Re-Globalization

The world is going through a process of re-globalization. In 2007, merely 16 years ago, American journalist Thomas Friedman's *The World Is Flat* described a world in which people, money, goods, and information cross political and geographical borders freely. The world was generally peaceful and engaged in trading. An increasing number of people were getting along and enjoying prosperity. Despite minor human conflicts in certain areas, there were no major wars between countries. All nations were involved in the third wave of globalization (Friedman, 2007).

Today, the world is drastically different. Ongoing tensions and armed hostilities are causing nations to align with allies to reinforce separatist lines and strongholds. Moreover, the relationship between China and the Western world is fractured with all sorts of tensions, from trade wars and political and economic sanctions to technological embargoes and military skirmishes. Nationalism and racism are on the rise across the globe. Anti-immigration is gaining momentum in different countries and travel across countries has declined. The global supply chain has been disrupted and is being reorganized along political lines.

The type of globalization seen in previous decades is no more. The world is going through a process of re-globalization. It is difficult to predict what the world will look like as we move forward. Things we thought we could count on as constants are in flux, political leaderships are changing, political systems are changing, ideologies are changing, and so are relationships among countries. We are not sure about geopolitics but we are sure that globalization is being reshaped and military spending is on the rise in many countries.

Although it is uncertain what the re-globalized world will be like, schools must prepare for it because today's students will not only enter the re-globalized world as citizens and workers but also need to create changes in that world. PISA now assesses for global competency. Every student should understand globalization, other cultures, and other countries, and develop the ability to communicate and interact with others. School leaders must find ways to help students stay connected globally, learn globally, and develop global competence (Reimers, 2009; Zhao, 2009).

Globalization not only affects the qualities of future citizens, but it also affects how schools teach. Via the internet, students can access videos, podcasts, lessons, and courses globally; they can also take part in courses live with instructors and students globally. Furthermore, they can start learning communities to collaborate on projects with students in other countries. Today, no matter where a student is located, they can learn globally.

Climate Change and the Environment

The natural environment has become increasingly less habitable for humanity. Extreme temperatures, floods, droughts, damaging storms, sea-level rises, drying rivers, deforestation, and desertification are just some of the visible examples.

These are global and local problems. There are no easy solutions that can quickly solve these problems. Moreover, any solution is a double-edged sword that delivers both good and bad outcomes. For example, carbon reduction is certainly good for limiting drastic climate change and pollution in the long run, but it requires changes in energy use that can significantly increase the price of production and thus add cost to goods. Solar and wind energy are greener, but they require new technology and equipment. The use of alternative energy reduces the need for fossil fuels, which is the economic cornerstone for some regions. The diminishing fossil fuel industry is causing economic hardship in those communities.

Climate change and environmental pollution have energized debates among different factions of political leaders, scientists, engineers, and businesses, but the overall tendency is to take collective action to change human behaviors. Young people have been vocal and active in this movement, and some have been highly influential, as in the case of Greta Thunberg. Many schools have environmental programs that engage students in actions to slow down climate change and make the environment cleaner. But there is much more schools can—and will need to—do. Students must live in the future and must develop the capabilities and mindset to find better solutions, whatever they may be, for a better earth; all of which requires new thinking now in schools around the world to ensure that there is hope and possibilities for our future generations.

Failure of Past Education Reforms

The Global Education Reform Movement, which Pasi Sahlberg shortened to GERM, has arguably not yet had the desired universal impact. This movement has not yet improved the overall quality of education and has not narrowed the achievement gap between advantaged and disadvantaged students. Moreover, students' social, psychological, and emotional well-being has been in decline and reached a critical level (Sahlberg, 2023; Zhao, 2021).

These failures have put great pressure on school leaders and education systems to reform and provide improved outcomes for all. Simply changing the curriculum and curriculum standards, holding teachers and school leaders more accountable, and constantly testing students do not make the difference required. What is needed is to rethink learning in the new age of technology and globalization. It is essential to consider students as purposeful, intentional, diverse, and natural learners who are the managers and owners of their own learning.

ChatGPT and AI, the COVID-19 pandemic, climate change, re-globalization, and the failure of education reforms are not the only emerging challenges for schools. Race, ethnicity, poverty, equity, religion, culture, and a host of other issues have already deeply affected human societies within and between countries. The world has become undeniably more uncertain (McDiarmid & Zhao, 2022). The uncertainty schools face is a great opportunity for change, but it can also be a great incentive for school leaders to try to return schools to the normalcy, certainty, and safety of the pre-pandemic world, which is actually only a fantasy.

> *What is needed is to rethink learning in the new age of technology and globalization. It is essential to consider students as purposeful, intentional, diverse, and natural learners who are the managers and owners of their own learning.*

Our view is that school leaders should embrace disruptions and crises by future-proofing their schools. There are no other options. Unless we ignore the abundance of evidence that education was very problematic prior to the pandemic, we cannot return to the way things were before—no matter how much we think we want to. We need to create a better future for schools.

SUGGESTED ACTION STEPS FOR LEADING FOR THE FUTURE: THE CHANGES WE MUST HAVE

High-performing school leaders must be future-focused and prepared to lead from the front. The school community needs to look to the immediate future to equip students with the tools, disposition, skills, and strength to make the necessary future-oriented changes. To start, consider the what and how of learning (Zhao & Watterston, 2021).

Question What Is Worth Learning: Make Humans More Human

In the middle of the Industrial Revolution, British philosopher Herbert Spencer wrote *What Knowledge Is of Most Worth* (Spencer, 1911), in which he argued that the classics and classical languages such as Latin and Greek were no longer of practical value. Instead, it was science that was of most worth in helping people become independent workers, parents, and productive citizens.

We now need to ask that question again. ChatGPT and other AI tools are predicted to disrupt high-paying jobs—those that require higher education—more than low-paying and low-skill jobs (Kelly, 2020; Muro et al., 2019). Goldman Sachs predicted that AI could replace about 300 million full-time jobs (Cox, 2023). AI and technology are developed to do things that humans do not like to do, do less well or less effectively, or cannot do. The disruption presents a great challenge to education: What should students learn if technology can do what schools teach students to do?

ChatGPT has already shown that it can do the tasks we try to teach our students to do and more. As AI becomes more sophisticated, the knowledge we teach students can be easily produced by technology. What should we teach so students are able to thrive? A smart strategy would be to not compete with technology but, instead, to use it to assist us in meeting the goals we have for our work and our lives.

Apple's CEO Tim Cook said in a 2018 interview,

> They're worried about machines taking jobs and AI sort of replacing humans. My worry is not that machines will think like people—it's that people will think like machines. And so that to me is a much bigger worry. (Fried, 2018)

The question future-oriented leaders must lead the entire school community to ponder is, are students being taught to think like machines? If so, what should be changed? To compete with smart machines or AI-driven technology, humans need to become more human rather than more mechanical. What makes humans more human? What are the major differences between human beings and AI technologies? What are the characteristics human beings have that machines, no matter how smart or sophisticated, do not have? Unlike machines, humans are problem finders, they are capable of creativity, they act with intentionality, they are social and emotional, and each individual human is unique from any other.

Humans have the unique capacity to identify problems before they know how to solve them (Zhao, 2022b). To survive and thrive, humans are in a constant process of identifying and solving small and big problems. In contrast, machines (so far) can only solve problems that have been supplied by humans.

Humans are creative (Baer, 2022; Florida, 2012; Weisberg, 2020). Human beings rely on creativity to find meaningful problems and reasonable solutions, but machines are unable to go beyond their algorithms to become creative, although they are great at developing answers and solutions with massive amounts of data.

Humans are intentional and purposeful. They take actions that follow their intentions, and their actions have purpose. Machines, even AI-driven machines, do not have intentions and purposes. They take actions in response to human purpose-driven actions. Only when humans initiate orders do machines take action.

Humans are social beings with very complex emotions. Machines, even AI-driven machines, are not capable of emotions nor are they social.

Finally, we humans are all unique. No two humans are identical because of the interactions between our innate conditions and our experiences in later life. Machines are not unique in the same way as human beings. AI tools, for example, can produce different responses to different questions raised by different people, but they fundamentally rely on the same set of data and coding, which ultimately limits their reactions and outputs.

To help develop humans who can thrive in the world of smart machines, schools need to shift the focus of education toward the development of characteristics that make us unique. School leaders must inspire everyone in their school communities to change their mindset: Education is not about imposing the same knowledge and skills on all students; instead, education needs to focus on helping every student to become uniquely great and to use their greatness to solve meaningful problems (Zhao, 2012, 2022b; Zhao & Tavangar, 2016). Lead teachers in your school to facilitate the development of a jagged profile of competence for each student. Through the profile, show how the student is unique, highlight their strengths, and develop a plan to help them build on those strengths. Committing to the development of a jagged profile requires educators and education systems to accept that students will not be equally adept in every area, but a unique, comprehensive, and rounded profile will identify achievements, capabilities, and dispositions that will recognize the abilities of and opportunities for each student.

These changes challenge the idea of a predetermined curriculum, one set of standards, and one standardized test meeting the needs of all students. To meet educational needs in the age of smart machines, schools must change the mindset that all students should learn the same thing, move at the same pace, and grasp all prescribed subjects. It also requires policymakers, educators, and parents to accept that not all prescribed content is valuable and that not all so-called "useless" talents are valueless (Zhao, 2019).

Question What Learning Is: Personalization Is the Only Way Forward

If schools are willing to accept that students must become unique and develop their human characteristics, they must change how learning is organized. Personalization of learning is not only necessary but also possible (Zhao, 2018b, 2018c, 2021). Each student must be treated as a unique individual with unique passions and strengths as well as weaknesses. All students should be recognized as intentional and purposeful human beings who are creative and have social and emotional needs. They also have the right of self-determination and they are capable of learning both in and out of the classroom (Watterston & Zhao, 2023; Wehmeyer & Zhao, 2020).

To change the organization of learning, schools should start by giving students the freedom to develop their own learning plans. Although every society and school provides students with common learning experiences so they can develop the knowledge and skills required of citizens, that should not be the extent of their education (Zhao, 2021). Imagine dividing school time into parts to cover both nationally/socially required content and local, school-defined content. Leave the remaining time up to students to decide what they want to learn and how they will learn it.

Giving students time and assistance to develop their own learning plans involves conversations with students and guardians. Talk about what each student is interested in learning and developing in passions such as the arts, sports, solving problems, and competency development. At the end of the conversation, you should have an emerging personalized learning plan that includes learning goals, resources, and support. The plan should be regularly reviewed and revised according to progress. It is possible that students may find new interests and new strengths that will change their plans. Teachers should be responsive to the desired changes and work with students and parents accordingly.

Create dedicated time for students to be engaged in personalized learning. Personalized learning is led by students and owned by students, with the guidance of a teacher facilitator assigned to groups of students. Note that the teachers' role involves supporting, managing, and assessing personalized learning outcomes for students as a component of their jagged profile. They can serve as coaches who help students identify and develop their interests and strengths, and as facilitators who help students find, evaluate, and learn from online resources (Zhao, 2018a, 2022a). It is, however, fundamental that students develop critical awareness and analytical ability as they use increasingly enticing technology and communication platforms, to ensure they are able to manage their own learning based on evidence, facts, and credible sources.

Help students use technology to develop new learning opportunities (Zhao, 2021). Technology has enabled a global distribution of learning resources in various media. There are courses on virtually any topic online and there are potential experts who are willing to help. Beyond YouTube, TikTok, and other video-sharing sites, there are Khan Academy, Coursera, Udemy, and other dedicated collections. There are also social media groups and online learning communities (Aragon et al., 2019). ChatGPT and other emerging AI tools will deliver more sophisticated, possibly individualized, and responsive learning content. Most students have not been prepared to learn from these resources despite their easy access and wide availability. Schools traditionally limit learning to what teachers offer in classrooms. To enable personalization of learning, schools should help students learn about new learning resources and create their own learning ecosystem (Zhao, 2021).

Personalization of learning does not mean that students with a personalized learning plan are isolated from others. The opposite is true. Students interact with each other, collaborate with each other, and learn from, with, and for each other. Collaboration is not limited to students in the same school but includes students and adults in other parts of the world and in the local community (Zhao, 2018c, 2021). To be successful, these collaborations need teacher facilitation, organization, and supervision. Teachers can also help by guiding students in developing the ability, mindset, and attitude needed for collaboration on a global scale.

This new way of learning is only possible when schools are willing to rethink the organization of learning. In this new paradigm, students would no longer be permanently organized into classes based on age or ability. Rather, they would be seen as individual, independent, and self-determined learners, and as the owners of their learning. Students need guidance and support from adult teachers, but they do not always have to sit in a classroom with their peers. They do not need adult teachers to supervise, manage, and lecture them all the time.

> *This new way of learning is only possible when schools are willing to rethink the organization of learning. In this new paradigm, students would no longer be permanently organized into classes based on age or ability. Rather, they would be seen as individual, independent, and self-determined learners, and as the owners of their learning.*

We must rethink how teachers work. If teachers have the time to work with students over the course of a year or at least a semester, they will have plenty of time to work one-on-one with students while other students are working independently. Because of the nature of personalized and independent learning, the teacher's time is much more flexible, allowing them to give more individualized time to each student.

Don't Wait for the System

School leaders must act now. They cannot and should not wait for system mandates, for other schools to change, or for a time when everyone is ready to change.

Whenever we talk about change, many school leaders note that the education system's mandated curriculum and assessments limit their ability to change. They ask when systems will make the changes so that they are able to change their schools. Waiting for systems to change is not an option for school leaders who need to make the change immediately. Systems have to be responsible for every student, every teacher, and every school, so they are unable to lead individual changes that work for some students, some teachers, and some schools. Moreover, it is very difficult for systems and system leaders to quickly develop a common understanding of and proper reactions to major and constantly developing events such as ChatGPT and AI.

School leaders should lead changes as appropriate and necessary in their own schools, within the confines of the system. No matter how constraining and controlling system requirements are, there are always possibilities for negotiated and evidence-based change. If the school team feels essential changes are needed, they need to invite students and community members to creatively imagine new ways of learning and teaching.

Don't Simply Copy

School leaders also ask, "Who else is making changes?" They want to visit other schools to see change in action with their own eyes. They want to seek confirmation that the changes are beneficial, and they want to learn from what others have done. There is nothing wrong with learning from or even copying others in the beginning, but we strongly advise leaders to lead changes uniquely tailored to the needs and goals of their school context. The catalyst for change should not be because others are making changes. The advancements of other schools can add confidence and possibly help convince the school community that changes are needed and can be made; however, the motivation for change should be that learning for all is improved. Finally, it is important for school leaders to believe that their teachers and students are creative and capable of developing their own changes. Effective school leaders always work with their own teachers, students, and local communities to imagine and create evidence-based changes that are appropriate for their own schools.

You Don't Make the Changes

Effective school leaders do not decide on changes in isolation and then impose them on teachers and students. Leaders empower, support, and encourage teachers and students to create and initiate changes. It should rarely (if ever) be the leader who initiates a program with the expectation that all teachers and students will follow.

Smart leaders work with teachers and students so that everyone understands why changes are needed. When teachers and students understand the *why*, they can create the *how* much better than the school leader because they are closer to the problems and the contexts than the school leader.

DEVELOPMENT AND FACILITATION OF RESPONSIVE CHANGES

All educational changes must be responsive to the future that our children will live in and contribute to. Future-proofed changes should be driven by these two major factors: dealing with the uncertain future and the changing contexts of education.

School leaders can build a future-proof school by building a future-oriented culture. In this culture, teachers are thinking about how to prepare students for an uncertain future. They are actively developing new ways of teaching for the new context of education. Students are also thinking about their future and how to shape the future for the benefit of all humanity. Moreover, they are actively seeking new ways of learning within the new context of education. Make it clear to all school staff and students that the school is about building a better future instead of fixing the past. This message needs to be repeated constantly because people will default to focusing on problems of the past and present instead of problems of the future.

Organize book studies. Each year, the entire school can read one book or a few articles or watch videos concerning the future of education or the changing context. Then the school can have meetings for staff and students to discuss the implications for their actions in the school. This can happen outside regular classes or can be implemented as part of the curriculum. The school can dedicate the first week to a schoolwide discussion of the book, articles, or videos. Such discussions can also include community members and system leaders.

Organize committees or task forces for the future made up of students and staff with strong interests in exploring new possibilities. These task forces can take on specific aspects of the school and imagine possible changes. For example, they can take on the entire school curriculum and imagine how it can be delivered to better prepare students for the uncertain future. They can also work on how to deliver the curriculum with new technologies and global resources.

The task forces can come up with specific proposals. The proposals can include potential changes, required budget, and resources, as well as benefits and possible side effects. These proposals can be disseminated to the entire school community for discussion and possible implementation. They can serve as great stimulation for considering the future and new possibilities in education.

The key to building a future-proof school lies with school leadership. It is up to the school leader to build the culture and to lead the teams to implement changes. But the school leader is not the teacher; they cannot be the one who actually implements the changes. The principal must understand that the teachers and students are the driving forces of change.

THE INNOVATOR'S DILEMMA

Before we end this chapter, we must discuss a common problem for school leaders: the innovator's dilemma. That is, the innovator often has a blind spot. They do not know what to focus on. They are so attached to their innovation that they believe that everything should stay as they have created even after they leave. We have heard school principals state that their successor has inherited the perfect school where everything operates so well that no change or improvement is needed. In secrecy, they hope that their successors are not as good as they are. They hope that they will not identify any opportunities for reform. It is as if they want the school preserved as a monument to their outstanding leadership and as a legacy to those who follow.

Leaders are important, but they are not the be-all and end-all. A school with strong teachers, students, and a healthy community of staff and parents can also identify new opportunities for growth and improvement. The legacy for high-performing and empowering school leaders is all about the prevailing culture and the density of leadership across the teaching staff who have agency and deep knowledge of how to collectively improve practice. If a school has experienced co-constructing a vision and the vision is shared across the many different groups of stakeholders, the school will continue to change and improve well after the current leader departs, as circumstances alter. The best legacy of all is a school that can adapt and respond no matter what the challenge because the staff team is united, capable, and empowered.

Think about sustainability. No matter how long you are in the school as a leader, you will eventually leave. The school conditions when you leave are the foundation for future leaders and future changes. When you work with teachers and other actors in the school, develop the talents and passions of everyone involved in the school. The changes do not belong to the leader or a few teachers or students; they belong to all involved in the school which is continually evolving.

CHAPTER 8 FOCUS POINTS

1. Schools are faced with tremendous challenges and crises. In these challenges and crises lie great opportunities. To prepare students to make meaningful contributions for a better future, school leaders must empower the teaching team to lead the change.

2. The most significant changes you will make will be why, what, when, and where to teach. Question the worthiness of the knowledge and skills schools provide for students to learn and the value of the one-size-fits-all educational approach. Help students develop capabilities that cannot be replaced by smart machines. Personalize learning for all students.

3. Do not wait for educational systems to initiate changes because systems do not respond fast enough. Do not wait for other schools to make changes because changes must be local. Do not make changes alone. Lead and empower the entire school to make changes together.

REFERENCES

Ainley, J., Macaskill, G., & Thomson, S. (2022). *Within and between school variation in achievement on the Programme for International Student Assessment (PISA) in Australia, PISA Australia technical paper*. Australian Council for Educational Research.

Ainley, R. (2019). *Lifting system performance through leadership development: Inspiration and challenge from health and education leaders*. Nous Group.

Aragon, C. R., Davis, K., & Fiesler, C. (2019). *Writers in the secret garden: Fanfiction, youth, and new forms of mentoring*. The MIT Press.

Australian Institute for Teaching and School Leadership (AITSL). (2014). *Australian professional standard for principals and the leadership profiles*. AITSL.

Australian Institute for Teaching and School Leadership (AITSL). (2016). *Interactive leadership profiles – Vision and values, Australian institute for teaching and school leadership*.

Australian Institute for Teaching and School Leadership. (2019). *Spotlight diversity in school leadership*.

Baer, J. (2022). *There's no such thing as creativity: How Plato and 20th century psychology have misled us*. Cambridge University Press. https://doi.org/10.1017/9781009064637

Beard, A. (2018). *Natural born learners: Our incredible capacity to learn and how we can harness it*. Hachette UK.

Beghetto, R. A. (2023). Broadening horizons of the possible in education. *Possibility Studies & Society*. https://doi.org/10.1177/27538699231182014

Beng, H., Morris, R., Gorard, S., Kokotsaki, D., & Abdi, S. (2020). Teacher recruitment and retention: A critical review of international evidence of most promising interventions. *Education Sciences, 10*(10), 262.

Bonawitz, E., Shaftob, P., Gweonc, H., Goodmand, N. D., Spelkee, E., & Schulzc, L. (2011). The double-edged sword of pedagogy: Instruction limits spontaneous exploration and discovery. *Cognition, 120*(3), 322–330.

Bohrnstedt, G., Kitmitto, S., Ogut, B., Sherman, D., & Chan, D. (2015). *School composition and the black–white achievement gap* [NCES 2015-018]. Retrieved from https://nces.ed.gov/nationsreportcard/pubs/studies/2015018.aspx

Bransford, J. D., Brown, A. L., & Cocking, R. R. (Eds.). (2000). *How people learn: Brain, mind, experience, and school*. The National Academies Press.

Brunello, G., & Schlotter, M. (2010). *The effect of noncognitive skills and personality traits on labour market outcomes*. http://www.epis.pt/downloads/dest_15_10_2010.pdf

Buchsbaum, D., Gopnik, A., Griffiths, T. L., & Shaftob, P. (2011). Children's imitation of causal action sequences is influenced by statistical and pedagogical evidence. *Cognition, 120*(3), 331–340.

Bush, T., & Glover, D. (2014). School leadership models: What do we know? *School Leadership & Management, 34*(5), 553–571.

Cooper, S. (2017). Teaching is a team sport. *Journal of General Music Education, 30*(3). https://doi.org/10.1177/1048371317694821

Cox, J. (2023). *AI anxiety: The workers who fear losing their jobs to artificial intelligence*. https://www.bbc.com/worklife/article/20230418-ai-anxiety-artificial-intelligence-replace-jobs

Dean, D., Jr., & Kuhn, D. (2007). Direct instruction vs. discovery: The long view. *Science Education, 91*(3), 384–397.

Dewey, J. (1916). *Democracy and education.* Free Press.

Duckworth, A. L., & Yeager, D. S. (2015). Measurement matters: Assessing personal qualities other than cognitive ability for educational purposes. *Educational Researcher, 44*(4), 237–251.

Ekoko, B. E., & Ricci, C. (2014). *Natural born learners: Unschooling and autonomy in education.* CreateSpace.

Elmore, R. (2016, January 18). *Reflections on the role of tutoria in the future of learning.* https://redesdetutoria.com/download/69/articulos/11392/reflections-on-role-of-tutoria.pdf

Emler, T. E., Zhao, Y., Deng, J., Yin, D., & Wang, Y. (2019). Side effects of large-scale assessments in education. *ECNU Review of Education, 2*(3), 279–296.

Fiarman, S. E. (2017). Building a schoolwide leadership mindset. *Educational Leadership: Lifting School Leader, 74*(8), 22–27.

Firestone, W. A., & Robinson, V. M. J. (2010). Research on educational leadership: Approaches/promising directions. In *International encyclopedia of education* (3rd ed., pp. 740–745). https://www.sciencedirect.com/referencework/9780080448947/international-encyclopedia-of-education

Florida, R. (2012). *The rise of the creative class: Revisited* (2nd ed.). Basic Books.

Fried, I. (2018, November 19). *Tim Cook discusses staying human in an AI world.* https://www.axios.com/tim-cook-apple-artificial-intelligence-human-ec98a548-0a2f-4a7a-bd65-b4d25395bc27.html

Friedman, T. L. (2007). *The world is flat: A brief history of the twenty-first century.* Farrar, Straus and Giroux.

Fullan, M. (2008). *The six secrets of change: What the best leaders do to help their organizations survive and thrive.* Jossey-Bass.

Fullan, M. (2014). *The principal: Three keys to maximizing impact.* Jossey-Bass.

Ginsberg, R., & Zhao, Y. (2023). *Duck and cover: Confronting and correcting dubious practices in education.* Teachers College Press.

Goldberg, L. R. (1993). The structure of phenotypic personality traits. *American Psychologist, 48*(1), 26–34.

Harris, A., & Jones, M. (2018). Why context matters: A comparative perspective on education reform and policy implementation. *Educational Research for Policy and Practice, 17*(3), 195–207.

Hattie, J. (2012). *Visible learning for teachers: Maximizing impact on learning.* Routledge.

Hattie, J. (2015). High impact leadership. *Educational Leadership, 72*(5), 36–40.

Hattie, J. (2023). *Visible learning: The sequel: A synthesis of over 2,100 meta-analyses relating to achievement.* Taylor & Francis.

Heifetz, R., & Linsky, M. (2002). *Leadership on the line: Staying alive through the dangers of leading.* Harvard Business School Press.

Hunter, J., Sonnemann, J., & Joiner, R. (2022). *Making time for great teaching: How better government policy can help.* Grattan Institute.

IPCC. (2022). *Climate change 2022: Impacts, adaptation and vulnerability. Contribution of working group II to the sixth assessment report of the intergovernmental panel on climate change* [H.-O. Pörtner, D. C. Roberts, M. Tignor, E. S. Poloczanska, K. Mintenbeck, A. Alegría, M. Craig, S. Langsdorf, S. Löschke, V. Möller, A. Okem, B. Rama (Eds.)]. Cambridge University Press. doi:10.1017/9781009325844

Ippolito, J., & Fisher, D. (2019). Instructional leadership for disciplinary literacy. *Educational Leadership: The Power of Instructional Leadership, 76*(6), 50–56.

Kapur, M. (2014). Productive failure in learning math. *Cognitive Science, 38*(5), 1008–1022.

Kapur, M. (2016). Examining productive failure, productive success, unproductive failure, and unproductive success in learning. *Educational Psychologist, 51*(2), 289–299.

Kapur, M., & Bielaczyc, K. (2012). Designing for productive failure. *Journal of the Learning Sciences, 21*(1), 45–83.

Kelly, J. (2020). *U.S. lost over 60 million jobs—Now robots, tech and artificial intelligence will take millions more.* Retrieved October 27, 2020, from https://www.forbes.com/sites/jackkelly/2020/10/27/us-lost-over-60-million-jobs-now-robots-tech-and-artificial-intelligence-will-take-millions-more/?sh=6b78ccb01a52

Kirtman, L., & Fullan, M. (2016). *Leadership: Key competencies for whole-system change.* Solution Tree Press.

Kise, J. A., & Watterston, B. K. (2019). *Step in, step up: Empowering women for the school leadership journey.* Solution Tree Press.

Klusmann, U., Aldrup, K., Roloff-Bruchmann, J., Carstensen, B., Wartenberg, G., Hansen, J., & Hanewinkel, R. (2023). Teachers' emotional exhaustion during the COVID-19 pandemic: Levels, changes, and relations to pandemic-specific demands. *Teaching and Teacher Education, 121*, 103908.

Kotter, J. (1999). *What leaders really do.* Harvard Press.

Lane, D. (2018). *Deschooling in school: Part 1.* https://www.self-directed.org/tp/deschooling-in-school/

Leithwood, K., Jantzi, D., & McElheron-Hopkins, C. (2006). The development and testing of a school improvement model. *School Effectiveness and School Improvement, 17*(4), 441–464.

Leithwood, K., Sun, J., & Pollock, K. (Eds.). (2017). *How school leadership influences student learning: The four paths.* Springer.

Levin, H. M. (2012). More than just test scores. *Prospects: The Quarterly Review of Comparative Education, 42*(3), 269–284.

Levin, S., & Engel, S. (2016). *A school of our own the story of the first student-run high school and a new vision for American education.* The New Press.

Lewis, J. M., Fischman, D., Riggs, I., & Wasserman, K. (2013). Teacher learning in lesson study. *The Mathematics Enthusiast, 10*(3), 583–620.

Lewontin, R. (2001). *The triple helix: Gene, organism, and environment.* Harvard University Press.

Loveless, T. (2006). *How well are American students learning?* https://www.brookings.edu/wp-content/uploads/2016/06/2015-Brown-Center-Report_FINAL.pdf

Luce, D. (1992). The principal as orchestral conductor. *Oregon School Study Council Report, 32(3).* https://files.eric.ed.gov/fulltext/ED348718.pdf

Lund, S., Madgavkar, A., Manyika, J., & Smit, S. (2020). *What's next for remote work: An analysis of 2,000 tasks, 800 jobs, and nine countries.* https://www.mckinsey.com/featured-insights/future-of-work/whats-next-for-remote-work-an-analysis-of-2000-tasks-800-jobs-and-nine-countries

Maslow, A. H. (1943). A theory of human motivation. *Psychological Review, 50*(4).

McDiarmid, G. W., & Zhao, Y. (2022). *Learning for uncertainty: Teaching students how to thrive in a rapidly evolving world.* Routledge.

McGaw, B., Louden, W., & Wyatt-Smith, C. (2020). *NAPLAN review: Final report.* https://naplanreview.com.au/pdfs/2020_NAPLAN_review_final_report.pdf

Mullis, I. V. S., Martin, M. O., & Loveless, T. (2016). *20 Years of TIMSS: International trends in mathematics and science: Achievement, curriculum, and instruction.* Retrieved from http://timssandpirls.bc.edu/timss2015/international-results/timss2015/wp-content/uploads/2016/T15-20-years-of-TIMSS.pdf

Muro, M., Whiton, J., & Maxim, R. (2019). *What jobs are affected by AI? Better-paid, better-educated workers face the most exposure.* https://www.brookings.edu/research/what-jobs-are-affected-by-ai-better-paid-better-educated-workers-face-the-most-exposure/

National Academies of Sciences, Engineering, and Medicine. (2018). *How people learn II: Learners, contexts, and cultures.* The National Academies Press.

OECD. (2012). *Equity and quality in education: Supporting disadvantaged students and schools.* OECD Publishing.

OECD. (2016). Overview: Excellence and equity in education. In *PISA 2015 results (Volume I): Excellence and equity in education.* https://doi.org/10.1787/9789264266490-5-en

OECD. (2018). *The future of education and skills: Education 2030.* Position Paper. http://www.oecd.org/education/2030/E2030%20Position%20Paper%20(05.04.2018).pdf

OECD. (2019). *PISA 2018 results (Volume III): What school life means for students' lives.* https://doi.org/10.1787/acd78851-en

OECD. (2020). Were schools equipped to teach e and were students ready to learn e remotely? *PISA in Focus*, No. 108. https://doi.org/10.1787/4bcd7938-en

Paine, L., & Ma, L. (1993). Teachers working together: A dialogue on organizational and cultural perspectives of Chinese teachers. *International Journal of Educational Research, 19*(8), 675–697.

Pelletier, K,. Robert, J., Muscanell, N., McCormack, M., Reeves, J., Arbino, N., Grajek, S., Birdwell, T., Liu, D., Mandernach, J., Moore, A., Porcaro, A., Rutledge, R., & Zimmern, J. (2023). *2023 EDUCAUSE horizon report, teaching and learning edition.* EDUCAUSE, 2023.

Peterson, P. L. (1979). Direct instruction: Effective for what and for whom. *Educational Leadership, 37*(1), 46–48.

Reddy, P., Sharma, B., & Chaudhary, K. (2020). Digital literacy: A review of literature. *International Journal of Technoethics (IJT), 11*(2), 65–94.

Reimers, F. (2009). Educating for global competency. In J. E. Cohen & M. B. Malin (Eds.), *International perspective on the goals of universal basic and secondary education* (pp. 183–202). Routledge.

Reiss, S. (2000). *Who am I? The 16 basic desires that motivate our behavior and define our personality.* Jeremy P. Tarcher/Putnam.

Reiss, S. (2004). Multifaceted nature of intrinsic motivation: The theory of 16 basic desires. *Review of General Psychology, 8*(3), 179–183.

Ridley, M. (2003). *Nature via nurture: Genes, experience, and what makes us human* (1st ed.). HarperCollins.

Robinson, V., Bendikson, L., McNaughton, S., Wilson, A., & Zhu, T. (2017). Joining the dots: The challenge of creating coherent school improvement. *Teachers College Record, 119*(8), 1–44.

Robinson, V., & Gray, E. (2019). What difference does school leadership make to student outcomes? *Journal of the Royal Society of New Zealand, 49*(2), 171–187.

Rose, T. (2016). *The end of average: How we succeed in a world that values sameness* (1st ed.). HarperOne.

Ryan, R. M., & Deci, E. L. (2017). *Self-determination theory: Basic psychological needs in motivation, development, and wellness.* Guilford Publications.

Sahlberg, P. (2010). Rethinking accountability in a knowledge society. *Journal of Educational Change, 11*(1), 45–63.

Sahlberg, P. (2023). Trends in global education reform since the 1990 s: Looking for the right way. *International Journal of Educational Development, 98,* 102748. https://doi .org/10.1016/j.ijedudev.2023.102748

Schleicher, A., Ed. (2012). *Preparing teachers and developing school leaders for the 21st century: Lessons from around the world.* OECD Publishing. http://dx.doi .org/10.1787/9789264xxxxxx-en

Seligman, M. E. P. (2002). *Authentic happiness: Using the new positive psychology to realize your potential for lasting fulfillment.* Free Press.

Sharratt, L., & Planche, B. (2016). *Leading collaborative learning: Empowering excellence.* Corwin.

Shulman, R. D. (2018, January 17). *Endorsed by entrepreneurs: How this high school teacher is making the classroom a safe place to fail.* https://www.forbes .com/sites/robynshulman/2018/01/17/ endorsed-by-entrepreneurs-how-this-high-school-teacher-is-making-the-classroom-a-safe-place-to-fail/?sh=581513663543

Spencer, H. (1911). What knowledge is of most worth. In H. Spencer (Ed.), *Essays on education and kindred subjects.* Dent/Aldine Press.

Toegel, G., & Barsoux, J. L. (2012). How to become a better leader. *MIT Sloan Management Review, 53*(3), 51–60.

The Wallace Foundation. (2013). *The school principal as leader: Guiding schools to better teaching and learning.* https://www .wallacefoundation.org/knowledge-center/ Documents/The-School-Principal-as-Leader-Guiding-Schools-to-Better-Teaching-and-Learning-2nd-Ed.pdf

Watterston, J., & Zhao, Y. (2023). Rethinking the time spent at school: Could flexibility improve engagement and performance for students and teachers? *Prospects.* https:// doi.org/10.1007/s11125-023-09638-9

Wehmeyer, M., & Zhao, Y. (2020). *Teaching students to become self-determined learners.* ASCD.

Weisberg, R. W. (2020). *Rethinking creativity: Inside-the-box thinking as the basis for innovation.* Cambridge University Press.

Ydesen, C., & Bomholt, A. (2020). Accountability implications of the OECD's economistic approach to education: A historical case analysis. *Journal of Educational Change, 21*, 37–57.

Zhao, Y. (2009). *Catching up or leading the way: American education in the age of globalization.* ASCD.

Zhao, Y. (2011). Students as change partners: A proposal for educational change in the age of globalization. *Journal of Educational Change, 12*(2), 267–279. https://doi.org/10.1007/s10833-011-9159-9

Zhao, Y. (2012). *World class learners: Educating creative and entrepreneurial students.* Corwin.

Zhao, Y. (2014). *Who's afraid of the big bad dragon: Why China has the best (and Worst) education system in the world.* Jossey-Bass.

Zhao, Y. (2015). A world at risk: An imperative for a paradigm shift to cultivate 21st century learners. *Society, 52*(2), 129–135.

Zhao, Y. (2016a). *Counting what counts: Reframing education outcomes.* Solution Tree Press.

Zhao, Y. (2016b). *The take-action guide to world class learners. Book 1: How to make personalization and student autonomy happen.* Corwin.

Zhao, Y. (2016c). *The take-action guide to world class learners. Book 2, How to "make" product-oriented learning happen.* Corwin.

Zhao, Y. (2016d). *The take-action guide to world class learners. Book 3, How to create a campus without borders.* Corwin.

Zhao, Y. (2018a). The changing context of teaching and implications for teacher education. *Peabody Journal of Education, 93*(3), 1–14.

Zhao, Y. (2018b). Personalizable education for greatness. *Kappa Delta Pi Record, 54*(3), 109–115.

Zhao, Y. (2018c). *Reach for greatness: Personalizable education for all children.* Corwin.

Zhao, Y. (2018d). *What works may hurt: Side effects in education.* Teachers College Press.

Zhao, Y. (2019). The rise of the useless: The case for talent diversity. *Journal of Science Education and Technology, 28*, 62–68. https://doi.org/10.1007/s10956-018-9743-3

Zhao, Y. (2020). Social learning and learning to be social: From online instruction to online education. *American Journal of Education, 127*(1), 137–142.

Zhao, Y. (2021). *Learners without borders: New learning pathways for all students.* Corwin.

Zhao, Y. (2022a). New context, new teachers, and new teacher education. *Journal of Technology and Teacher Education, 30*(2), 127–133.

Zhao, Y. (2022b). Teaching students to identify and solve problems. *Principal Connections, 26*(2), 52–53.

Zhao, Y., Emler, T. E., Snethen, A., & Yin, D. (2019). *An education crisis is a terrible thing to waste: How radical changes can spark student excitement and success.* Teachers College Press.

Zhao, Y., & Tavangar, H. S. (2016). *World class learners: Personalized education for autonomous learning and student-driven curriculum.* Corwin.

Zhao, Y., & Watterston, J. (2021). The changes we need: Education post COVID-19. *Journal of Educational Change, 22*(1), 3–12. https://doi.org/10.1007/s10833-021-09417-3

Zhao, Y., Wehmeyer, M., Basham, J., & Hansen, D. (2019). Tackling the wicked problem of measuring what matters: Framing the questions. *ECNU Review of Education, 2*(3), 262–278.

Zhao, Y., Zhang, G., Lei, J., & Qiu, W. (2015). *Never send a human to do a machine's job: Correcting the top 5 mistakes in edtech.* Corwin.

INDEX

accountability processes, 19, 108, 112, 117
   contemporary, 109
achievements, 33, 37–38, 65, 96, 106, 126
actors, 7, 12, 39–40, 81, 91, 131
adopters, early, 70
advisors, 82–83
agreements, 20, 41, 44–45, 49–50, 86
AI (artificial intelligence), 4, 119–122, 125–126
alignment, 23–24, 42, 53, 55
Australian Institute for Teaching and School
   Leadership, 17, 48, 115

bureaucracies, 6, 14, 17, 20, 26, 33, 39,
   106, 111–12

ChatGPT, 4, 59, 100, 119–22, 124–25, 128–29
China, 59, 75, 121–22
climate change, 4, 34, 61, 120, 123–24
coaches, 1, 18, 21, 23, 25–26, 46, 82–83, 127
coaching, 15–16, 19, 21, 25
cognitive abilities, 62, 65–66
collaboration, 7, 18, 49, 68, 84, 91, 93, 113,
   116, 128
colleagues, 25, 38, 51, 64, 91–92, 111
community builders, 101
community leaders, 29, 106
community service and out-of-school learning, 114
compassion, 90
conductor principal, 18–19, 93
confidence, 18, 50–51, 64–66, 68–69, 92, 106,
   112, 114, 129
confident, 3, 45, 65–66, 79, 93
conflicts, 37, 62, 64, 66
connectors, global, 101
constructive change, 3, 91, 98, 121
contexts, changing, 130
countries, 2, 43, 53, 60, 97, 100, 105, 122–24
COVID-19 pandemic, 26, 32, 35–36, 47, 76,
   90, 121, 124

creative school leaders, 61
creativity, 26, 64–65, 68–69, 76, 95, 113, 126
credible school leader, 38
cultural change, 23
   sustained, 48
culture
   school's, 50
   student-centered, 97
curiosity, 64, 69, 79–80, 107
curricular flexibility, 60–61
curriculum, mandated, 60–61, 81, 129
customers, 32–34, 58

democratic school, student-centered, 84
density of leadership, 15, 45, 52, 131
disadvantaged students, 81, 124
disengaged students, 30, 82
drive, 2, 26, 39, 49, 54, 107, 112–13, 116

ecosystem, 13–14, 43, 128
education
   evidence-based, 120
   high-quality, 30, 37
   student-centered, 76
empowerment, 15–18, 23, 35, 53, 76,
   83, 88, 96–97
enablers, 17, 26, 37, 39, 101
evaluative culture, 115
evidence-based changes, 129
expectations of students and staff, 31
external stakeholders, 15, 21, 28, 40, 44–45, 50, 53
external systems, 26, 109

failures, productive, 63–64, 93
families, 5, 42–43, 52, 79–80, 106
fear, 30, 107–8, 111, 116–17
feedback, 49, 84, 94, 96, 102, 107, 109–10, 115
flipping, 27–28
formative accountability, 4, 18, 108, 115, 117

game plan, 1, 41–53, 55, 70, 97, 115
    school's, 49–50, 91
globalization, 4, 81, 101, 122–24
government-led innovations and changes, 90

hierarchy, 16, 27–29, 34, 40, 109
hierarchy of influence, 28–29, 31–32
high-performing school leaders, 3, 12, 16–17,
    25, 37, 45, 71, 98, 125
high-performing schools, 1, 38, 40, 82, 93–94
high-profile school leaders, 5
high-quality learning experience, 35–36
home, work from, 58–59, 79, 85, 121

ICEE (Innovation, Creativity, and
    Entrepreneurship Education), 59, 75
improvement, sustainable, 53, 94
improving student test scores, 67
Indooroopilly State School, 53
influence, 3, 7, 11, 14–16, 20, 27–35, 37,
    39–40, 45
influencers, 14, 27, 30, 32–33
    external, 28, 30, 33, 40
Innovation, Creativity, and Entrepreneurship
    Education (ICEE), 59, 75
innovation
    emerging, 98
    government-led, 90
innovation and improved student outcomes, 97
inspiration, 99, 120
instructional outcomes, 62, 64–66, 71
intelligent accountability, 111
intentions, 14, 50, 69, 126
internal school review teams, 112
invention, 57
invention education, 57
inverted triangle, 33, 39–40
inverted triangle of influence, 27, 29, 31–33,
    35, 37, 39

leaders
    educational, 20
    external, 14, 27, 32, 37, 51
    high-performing, 16, 36–38, 45, 70, 99
    key, 37, 51
    new, 28, 36, 46
    progressive, 119
    school-empowering, 28
    system-level, 70
leaders and influencers, 14, 32

leadership
    authentic student, 83
    evidence-based, 120
leadership and teamwork, 51
leadership model, 20–21
leadership practices, 21, 48
leadership responsibilities, 22
leadership styles, 14–15
leadership teams, 22–23, 29
    collaborative, 20
    empowered, 18, 21
    empowered high-functioning, 17
    empowered internal, 22
    empowered school, 20
    quality school, 21
leadership work, 25
learners
    born, 78
    diverse, 78, 81
    intentional, 78, 88
learning community, 2, 42, 45, 53, 55, 94, 101
learning ecosystem, 128
learning environment, 78, 90
learning outcomes, 102, 115, 122
    personalized, 127
learning plans, 82, 86, 127
learning process, 28, 59, 62, 83
learning programs, 16, 84
learning resources, 85, 101, 121, 128
levels, 7, 13–14, 22, 28, 49, 84, 96, 111, 116
lived experience, 7
long-term learning, 64
long-term outcomes, 62–64, 68

machines, 81, 125–26
meaningful problems, 59–60, 126
meetings, 6, 49, 57, 66, 92–93, 111,
    113, 125, 130
mentoring, 15–16, 19, 23, 25, 53, 90
model, team-based contemporary, 20
music, 18–19, 63, 79, 93

new age school leader, 30
new context, 63, 100–102, 130
noncognitive abilities, 65–66

OECD (Organization for Economic
    Co-operation and Development),
    2, 4, 15–16, 66, 81, 90
offend, 45

offices, 15, 25, 37–38, 110

orchestra, 19–21, 93

Organization for Economic Co-operation and Development. *See* OECD

out-of-school learning, 114

owners, 35, 76, 81–82, 101, 124, 128

pandemic, 121–22, 124

participation, student leadership, 114

peer tutoring, 87

performance, academic, 75, 95

performance improvement, local school, 113

personalities, 14, 33–34, 78–80, 111

personalization, 4, 21, 37, 101, 127–28

personalized learning, 82–83, 127

personalized learning outcomes for students, 127

PISA (Program for International Student Assessment), 60, 66, 123

policies, system-level, 31

policymakers, 5, 14, 19, 27, 29, 33, 38–40, 127

pressure, 25, 98, 108

principals, 5–6, 11–12, 16–20, 23, 107, 111–12

priorities, 30, 37, 44–45

   strategic, 52, 112

problem-based learning, 63

problems, real-world, 61, 65

problem-solving students, 62

process, audit, 110

process of empowerment, 96–97

productive culture, 11

productive culture of learning, 11

professional learning, 52, 54, 63, 113

profile

   jagged, 80, 88, 126–27

   school's leadership, 20

Program for International Student Assessment (PISA), 60, 66, 123

program of student performance improvement, 110

quality, 30, 33, 35–37, 82, 86

regional offices, 27, 33, 37–39, 54, 70

re-globalization, 120, 122–24

regulations, 1, 37–39, 77

relationships, 13, 15, 24, 31–32, 71, 78, 92–94, 96, 115, 122–23

resource curators, 82, 101

responsibilities, 1–2, 14, 21, 35, 37, 83, 86, 114–15

review processes, 107, 110, 112, 117

roles and responsibilities, 1–2, 114–15

rules, 84–85

school accountability, 77, 117

school boards, 28, 83, 108, 111

school community, local, 7

school culture, 1, 23, 33, 42, 46, 49, 57, 82, 94, 96

   improving, 42

school ecosystem, 29, 32

   local, 1

school improvement, 27, 42–43, 54, 105, 109, 111

school improvement processes, 53

school leader

   innovative, 119

   successful, 43, 64

school leadership

   contemporary, 16

   effective, 5–7, 12

   great, 13

   high-performance, 14

   high-performing, 15

   successful, 14, 91

school operations, 29, 84, 120

school performance, 12, 21, 33, 42, 44–45, 55, 106, 108, 112

school policies, 84, 122

school practices, 28, 45, 113, 120

school principals, 5, 11, 14, 17, 29, 33, 45, 81, 89, 131

school reforms, 77, 90, 94

school resources, 29, 83

school review, 112, 116–17

school's improvement plan, 1, 114

school systems, 19, 23, 32, 47, 109–10

school team, 53, 112, 129

self-determination, 35, 64–65, 68, 91–92, 100, 127

self-managed student learning, 99

services for special education students, 37

shared accountability, 21, 114

solving problems, 2, 21, 57–59, 61–63, 65, 68–69, 127

space and agency, 96–97

special education students, 37

staff

   disengaged, 50

   new, 49–50

   school's, 16

staff agency, 99

staff engagement, 47

staff meetings, after-school, 41
standardized tests, 30, 62, 66–67, 80, 82, 99, 117
strengths, 2, 50, 75, 79–80, 82–83, 101, 111, 125–27
stress, 47, 108, 111
student agency, 31, 83, 114
student engagement, 61, 83, 96, 98, 114
student-led discovery learning, 96
student-led learning, 86
student outcomes, 53, 55
student participation, 83–84
student performance, 70, 96, 99, 106, 110, 117
student progress, 98, 106
student success, 106
system leaders, 5, 27, 29–30, 32–33, 40, 51, 98, 109, 129–30
    educational, 27, 33
system-level leaders and staff, 70

talents, 19, 59–60, 78–79, 81–82, 90, 92, 131
task forces, 5, 130
teacher agency, 41, 47, 91
team-based contemporary model of school leadership, 20
teams, empowered, 17, 21

teamwork, 11, 51, 84, 93, 116
technology, 4, 58–59, 83, 85, 100, 113, 119–22, 125, 128
test scores, standardized, 30, 67
thinking, 47, 65, 69, 91, 119–20, 130
transition, contemporary school leadership, 21
triangle of influence, 27–28, 31, 39

uncertainty, 5, 55, 57–58, 121
understanding, clear, 7, 38, 71

vision, 12, 16, 40, 90–91, 94–96, 102, 131
voices, 35, 41, 46, 84, 92

work, challenging, 48, 93
work from home, 58–59, 79, 85, 121
workers, 2, 58–59, 121, 123
workloads, 1, 47, 52, 83
    overwhelming, 47, 97
world
    changing, 47, 71, 81
    new, 80–81, 113
    real, 58–60
    re-globalized, 123
world of uncertainty, 57–58

Helping educators make the greatest impact

CORWIN HAS ONE MISSION: to enhance education through intentional professional learning.

We build long-term relationships with our authors, educators, clients, and associations who partner with us to develop and continuously improve the best evidence-based practices that establish and support lifelong learning.

Solutions YOU WANT | Experts YOU TRUST | Results YOU NEED

INSTITUTES

Corwin Institutes provide regional and virtual events where educators collaborate with peers and learn from industry experts. Prepare to be recharged and motivated!

corwin.com/institutes

ON-SITE PROFESSIONAL LEARNING

Corwin on-site PD is delivered through high-energy keynotes, practical workshops, and custom coaching services designed to support knowledge development and implementation.

www.corwin.com/pd

VIRTUAL PROFESSIONAL LEARNING

Our virtual PD combines live expert facilitation with the flexibility of anytime, anywhere professional learning. See the power of intentionally designed virtual PD.

www.corwin.com/virtualworkshops

CORWIN ONLINE

Online learning designed to engage, inform, challenge, and inspire. Our courses offer practical, classroom-focused instruction that will meet your continuing education needs and enhance your practice.

www.corwinonline.com

Visit www.corwin.com

CORWIN

WHAT YOUR COLLEAGUES ARE SAYING . . .

This book challenges and inspires leaders to maximize their impact. Its pages will be well-worn as school leaders worldwide eagerly grasp its profound insights. The book reflects the authors' deep understanding of students' needs and offers a road map for leaders to meet those needs with unwavering dedication.

—**Emily McCarran**, **Head of Keystone Academy**
Beijing, China

Focused: Understanding, Negotiating, and Maximizing Your Influence as a School Leader is an enlightening, informative, and inspirational road map for any aspiring or experienced school leader; it tackles the seemingly overwhelming challenges of leaders providing guidance and—even more important—well-grounded reasons for hope in our profession.

—**Gabriel Rshaid**, **Co-Founder and Director, The Global School**
Founder and Director, The Learnerspace
Buenos Aires, Argentina

Watterston and Zhao have given hope to school leaders looking to transform their schools. This book gives concrete suggestions on how leaders can work with students, staff, and the larger community to bring about changes now. School leaders will be energized by these ideas to improve students' experiences and their schools.

—**Chris Kennedy**, **Superintendent of Schools**
West Vancouver, Canada

Focused shares a clear vision of where education needs to head and how leadership roles will need to change to meet that vision. This book successfully integrates research, stories from the field, and a blend of current reality with future focus.

—**Ellen Perconti**, **Superintendent**
Goldendale School District
Goldendale, Washington

Watterston and Zhao articulate ways to rethink leadership—for principals and teacher leaders. The impact on students will be significant.

—**Peter Dillon**, **Superintendent**
Berkshire Hills Regional School District
Stockbridge, Massachusetts